The BASIC Cookbook
By Ken Tracton

Radio Shack®
A DIVISION OF TANDY CORPORATION

FIRST EDITION

Library of Congress Cataloging in Publication Data

Tracton, Ken.
    The BASIC cookbook.

    Includes index.
    1. Basic (Computer program language) I. Title.
QA76.73.B3T7   001.6'424   78-4578
ISBN 0-8306-9901-5
ISBN 0-8306-1005-3 pbk.

Preface

BASIC was originally developed by John Kemeny and Thomas Kurtz in the 1960's at Dartmouth College. The ease of use and the simplicity of learning BASIC was noticed by various time-sharing services, who then started to implement BASIC for the use of their customers. BASIC now is no longer so basic, as there are many versions that are quite advanced. This book covers all the functions presently available on the majority of BASIC language versions, elementary or advanced. The user of this book can become adapted to any version of BASIC with little difficulty.

If you're in a computer course, you will be taught how to program in BASIC or a similar language. If, however, you have purchased a microcomputer, you will either receive with it a guide to programming of some kind or be referred to such a guide. The intention of this text is to give you a dictionary of terms used in BASIC with examples to illustrate all the functions and operations, as well as such mode and system commands as LOAD, RUN, SAVE and LIST.

Each statement, command or function, is provided with examples and, where deemed necessary, a programming example and a flowchart have been included.

I believe that once a fundamental understanding is reached on how the different statements and functions operate, the diligent user will be in a position to start exploring the multi-uses of BASIC. Also, since all the functions are in alphabetical order, this text may be used as a reference guide when using different versions of this common language.

If you already know the BASIC of your machine, you may find many terms which are missing from either your version of BASIC or from this text. Terms missing from this text are usually non-standard or "machine dependent" instructions, and you should rely on the guide that comes with your computer. Terms that are missing from your version of BASIC, and are in this text, are either synonyms, different ways of doing the same function, or have been left out for some reason.

I would like to thank David and Susan who drew the flowcharts from my sketched diagrams and repeatedly questioned me on what I was doing. I would also like to thank MITS (creator of the Altair) in the generous use of a model 680 computer, which proved to be a very useful tool in testing many of the programs.

I especially appreciate the advice Doreen and Owen gave me, and their invaluable help.

I wish to express my gratitude to Ms. Jane Hunt who took the time to decipher and decode my barely readable notes and to type the original manuscript. Without her time and patience this text would never have been finished.

Ken Tracton

Contents

Introduction...7

A Dictionary of BASIC Programming 17

Appendices 135
  Derived Functions 135
  Diagnostics (Common) 136
  Increase Program Speed 137
  Saving Space 137
  Speed (Processing) 138

Index..139

Introduction

What Is A Computer?

Think of a computer as a super-duper calculator. If you just turn the calculator on, nothing will happen. In order for a calculator to operate, you must feed in numbers and operations. An *operation* is an instruction to your calculator to perform a function: add, divide, find the square root, etc. For a computer, however, we must also instruct the computer to accept the numbers and to perform the operations.

If computers could work only with numbers, we would not need them; programmable calculators would be adequate for almost all our calculation needs. However, a computer can also work on *alphanumerics,* which are all the characters on your keyboard: the letters, the numbers, the punctuation marks and the signs above the numbers.

What Is A Program?

A *program* may be defined as a set of directions that tell a computer how to solve a problem. Any program may be considered to have three parts:

1. The necessary information, the *input data.*
2. The processing of the input data.
3. The *output*, results obtained from the processing.

These instructions must be written in a language which is understood by the computer.

Of all the high-level computer languages that have been written since 1955, BASIC (Beginner's All-purpose Symbolic Instruction Code) is definitely one of the easiest to learn. The simplicity of this language is actually quite deceiving as it possesses sufficient power and flexibility to solve a wide variety of problems. BASIC is available on most time-sharing large computer systems as well as being the number one language of the microcomputers.

The instructions in BASIC resemble algebraic formulae and include English statements. Since its structure is well suited for algebraic manipulation, BASIC is very useful for problem solving in science, mathematics, and engineering; but it is also used in many areas of numeric or character manipulation, such as medicine, psychology, economics, and business.

BASIC AS A CALCULATOR

Most versions of BASIC have a type of operation called *direct entry*. If you enter an operation without a line number, the operation is performed immediately and the answer is printed if the word PRINT precedes the operation.

The following are examples of direct entry and your fundamental functions. The first statement is your one line program; the number below is the computer output.

PRINT 5 + 6
11

PRINT 7*11
77

PRINT 39/13
3

PRINT SIN (.785398)
0.7071

PRINT LOG (20)
2.99573

PRINT SQR (2)
1.41421

PRINT 23*34.8
800.4

```
PRINT INT (45/8)
5

PRINT ABS (−9)
9

PRINT RND
0.9463

PRINT RND
0.2166
```

Note that each call to RND will produce a uniquely different random number.

These fundamental operations may be combined to produce complex results with ease. When combining operations, all expressions follow standard computer hierarchy of operations, and the computer will calculate:

First: Exponentiation ↑ or ▲ (in some basics **)
Second: Multiplication *
       Division /
Third: Addition +
     Subtraction −

When two operators belong to the same group

Example: 5 + 3 − 4
       6*7/2

the computer reads from left to right and performs the operations from left to right.

Example: (5 + 3) − 4
      (6 * 7)/2

HOW DO I WRITE A PROGRAM?

A complete BASIC program consists of an ordered sequence of statements, each instruction being written as a separate statement. These statements *must* appear in the order in which they are to be executed unless a deliberate transfer of control is indicated, for example, a subroutine.

The following rules always apply:

1) Every statement must appear on a separate line, unless the version allows multiline statements.
2) A statement cannot exceed one line in length, unless the version of BASIC being used has multi-line statements.
3) Each statement must begin with a positive integer quantity, called the statement number or line number.

4) No two statements may have the same line number.

5) Successive statements must have increasing (ascending) line numbers.

6) Each statement must contain a BASIC keyword, except versions of BASIC which do not require the LET keyword.

7) Blank spaces may be inserted anywhere desired in order to improve the readability of the statements.

Now let us examine a program named GUESS, written in BASIC that illustrates the fundamental concepts in this language. This program was chosen primarily because it contains no "bells or whistles" belonging to a SUPER BASIC program. The more esoteric statements and commands are covered in detail elsewhere in this text.

A BASIC PROGRAM

```
LOAD,GUESS
READY
LIST

10    REM THIS PROGRAM DEMONSTRATES BASIC
20    REM THE LINES 30 AND 40 ASK FOR A RANDOM
         NUMBER
30    PRINT "ENTER ANY NUMBER FROM 1 TO 100"
40    INPUT X
50    REM LINE 60 EVALUATES A RANDOM NUMBER
60    X = INT(X*RND)
70    REM THE FOLLOWING LINES ACCEPT THE GUESSES
80    PRINT "YOUR GUESS IS";
90    INPUT Y
100   IF Y = X THEN 200
110   IF Y>X THEN 300
120   PRINT "YOUR GUESS IS TOO LOW"
130   GOTO 80
200   PRINT "YOU HAVE GUESSED  CORRECTLY THE
         RANDOM NUMBER"
210   STOP
300   PRINT "YOUR GUESS IS TOO HIGH"
310   GOTO 80
320   END
READY
RUN
ENTER ANY NUMBER FROM 1 TO 100
```

? 50
YOUR GUESS IS ? 65
YOUR GUESS IS TOO LOW
YOUR GUESS IS ? 100
YOUR GUESS IS TOO HIGH
YOUR GUESS IS ? 75
YOUR GUESS IS TOO LOW
YOUR GUESS IS ? 80
YOU HAVE GUESSED CORRECTLY THE RANDOM NUMBER

END

Let us look at what has happened, and how this program in BASIC operated, We stated with the *command* LOAD, GUESS which instructed the computer to search its library for the program named GUESS. Where the program was stored is not of importance; it may have been on disc or on tape. Once the stored program was found it was transferred to the main memory of the computer.

When the computer was ready to accept another command it printed READY. A computer, while very fast, can only do one operation at a time. When it is free from a task it will notify the user by some message, usually the words GO or READY. We next typed in the command LIST, which instructed the computer to print out the program now residing under the name "GUESS" in main memory.

We list a program to verify that we have entered the right program instructions or to make corrections to an already written program. We do not have to list a program first to RUN it. After the computer had listed the program GUESS it again printed the READY message to indicate that it was waiting for a user command.

Typing the command RUN instructed the computer to start processing the program.

Looking through the program we notice the words REM at lines 10, 20, 50 and 70. The REM statement allows the programmer to add *REM*arks to a program. Whenever the computer reads a line beginning with the work REM, it does not process that line. Only during listing is a REM line evaluated.

One purpose of the REM statement is to enable the user to add useful information concerning the program when it is read or listed in the future. Quite often in long programs a user will forget why he wrote a certain line in a certain fashion. The REM removes this problem. Of course the REM statement is also useful for users other than the original programmer who wish to understand what a certain line does.

In line 30 we notice the word PRINT. The PRINT statement prints all characters that are enclosed in quotation marks following the word PRINT. The PRINT statement thus allows the program to output information, words or numbers. Whenever we wish to print anything in BASIC we use the PRINT statement.

The INPUT statement in line 40 tells the computer to ask for a number and assign the number then given by the user to the variable named X in this case. In line 90 the number is assigned to the variable Y. The INPUT statement allows us to *input* or enter information into the computer.

Line 60 (X = INT(X*RND)) constructed a random unber from the number entered by the user in line 40. The word RND is an instruction which tells the computer to pick a random number from 0 to 1 such as 0.96784. We then multiplied the number we entered by the random number. Since we are only interested in having an integer number in this program, we used the INT instruction which tells the computer to only use the integer part of a number. The resulting random integer number is assigned to the variable X. Whenever we assign a number to a variable that has been already used, the former number is lost.

In lines 100 and 110 we test to see if the number entered as a guess is in fact the random number. Line 100 tests whether the number is equal or not. If it is equal, we branch or go to line 200. If the test is false, Y is greater or less than X, and the next line, 110, is executed. Line 110 checks whether the number is greater than X. If it is, we go to line 300; if it is not, the next line is executed and prints a message saying we are too low in our guess. If Y = X and line 200 were executed, the "correct" message would be printed, and the next line encountered would be the STOP instruction which instructs the computer to stop program execution and END.

The END statement at the "end" of the program in line 320 tells the computer that this is the end of the program and that it should stop execution and await another user command. All BASIC programs must conclude with an END statement.

It should be obvious by now that the *execution* of the lines is sequential, going from lowest line number to highest line number. The only mechanisms that have disturbed this flow are the GOTO, and THEN instructions in lines 100, 110, 130 and 310.

The user may try this "basic" BASIC program and get the feel for this language. Reading the text the reader will find that writing in BASIC is much simpler than he expected. It is definitely "people-oriented." It does not require an extensive training in mathematics or programming.

BASIC programs are also very easy to alter. Once written, a program may be easily modified to suit other applications.

Because most BASICs are so similar, a program written on one machine will usually run on another computer, except for a few minor differences that may exist from one version to the next.

GOOD PRACTICE HINTS IN BASIC

1) Use REMs for documentation whenever possible.
2) Increment line number by 10, leaving space for future updates.
3) Write only one statement per line.
4) Try to avoid the special features available only on your version of BASIC.
5) Use I, J, K for index or counting variables throughout the program.
6) Use L, M, N for the end points or loops (FOR I = 1 TO M)
7) Avoid the letter O as a variable as confusion is inevitable with zero, whether your computer slashes the letter O or the zero.
8) Unless tight for space, do not reuse variable names.

BASIC and Computer Systems

BASIC is usually run on computers that operate in one of the following three modes:

A) Stand-alone
B) Time-sharing
C) BATCH

STAND-ALONE

In the stand-alone mode the computer is dedicated to only one user. That is, only one job or program is being run until completion. Generally the large computer systems are not stand-alone as it is not economically feasible to dedicate a large system to a single user.

Typical single-user machines are the host of microcomputers now available, and some of the specialized minicomputers.

The advantage, of course, of single-user, stand-alone operation is that the user has full command of the computer.

TIME-SHARING

In the time-sharing mode the computer is used "simultaneously" by more than one user. Each user can communicate with the computer via an input/output terminal which may be a teleprinter, video terminal or a combination of both.

The program and data are entered via the user's terminal and the results are returned to that terminal after processing.

There are many ways time-sharing may be effected by a computer. The system may take advantage of the slow response time of terminals and process data while the terminals are transmitting or receiving information. The system may also time-slice the users, that is, each user is allotted a time slot, and is polled in a round-robin method. Each user may be given 100 milliseconds of computer time, for example, then the next, and the next, and so on, until the computer returns to the original user. If the time slots are small and there are few users, each user views the system as being dedicated solely to his job.

BATCH

In the BATCH mode a number of jobs (programs) are entered into the computer and are processed sequentially. Typically this operational mode is done with punched cards, with both the program and data being recorded on these cards. A punched card typically contains 80 columns, of which some or all may contain holes. The pattern of holes in each column encodes the data, information, or instructions. Since each column represents one character, a single card can hold up to 80 characters of information. The cards are punched on special "card punches," then read into the computer by a card-reading device. The output of the program will then be printed on a line printer or, if graphics are being handled, on a plotter.

The advantage of the BATCH mode is that extremely large programs and quantities of data can be transmitted into and out of the computer very quickly. Therefore the BATCH mode is well suited for jobs that require large quantities of computer processing time or are physically long in length.

The serious drawback is that even if a given program requires only a few seconds of computer time, it may be resident within the system for a few hours to many days. Each job must wait until its turn has come up. Jobs are served on a first-in, first-to-be-processed basis. Thus for simple jobs the BATCH method is definitely undesirable.

THE AVAILABILITY OF BASIC

BASIC is now available as a compiler, translator, or interpreter. An interpreter stores in memory exactly what the user has entered. Upon execution the interpreter scans each line of code, translates the code into computer machine language (the fundamental machine codes the particular computer understands) and then executes the machine language image of the line. This sequence must be done for each line. Whether any given line has been interpreted once already is unimportant. The language does not store the machine code image. Thus in the event of a line being used ten times, it must be interpreted ten times.

A translator stores not the entered lines but rather a coded version of the input material. This coded version must still be interpreted but, because it is coded by function, it saves space and offers an increase in speed. Whether for interpretation or translation, the full BASIC language package must reside in memory.

A compiler compiles or "images" the total program as opposed to line by line into machine code. Thus even if a line is used ten times it is only compiled once. The total compiled image is stored in memory and is called an object program as opposed to a source program which is the original material. A compiler offers dramatic speed increases, and only requires a portion of the language package to remain in memory. This portion of compiler BASIC is called the run-time module. The run-time module effectively executes the BASIC compiled program.

The ability to run the same BASIC program on different machines is because, whether the version of BASIC is a translator, interpreter, or compiler, the end result is machine language. A version of BASIC written for one machine will use the instruction set of that computer to duplicate the functions of a BASIC written for another computer (machine language programs cannot be transferred from computer to computer).

If you are unfamiliar with BASIC programming, the entries listed below will give you a working knowledge of the language:

Argument	Hierarchy
Array	INPUT
Assignment	INT
CLEAR	Library Functions
Conditional Branching	Line Numbers
COS	LIST
END	Loops
Files	MARGIN
FOR-TO	Multiline Functions
GOSUB	Multiple Branching
GOTO	Nested Loops

NOT
Numbers
ON GO-SUB
OR
PI
PRINT
PRINT USING
Program
RANDOMIZE
REM
RETURN
RND

RUN
SCRATCH
SGN
SIN
SPACE$
SQR
STOP
String
Subroutine
Subscripted Variables
TAN
Variables

A Dictionary of BASIC Programming

● **ABS:** The library function ABS returns the absolute value of the expression within the parentheses that follow the keyword ABS.

EXAMPLES:

```
10    Y = ABS(J)
20    K = ABS(J-2)
30    PRINT ABS(A1)
```

PROGRAMMING EXAMPLE:

```
10    REM THIS PROGRAM DEMONSTRATES THE
20    REM ABS FUNCTION
30    PRINT "INPUT ANY NUMBER"
40    INPUT K
50    LET K = ABS(K)
60    PRINT LOG(K)
70    GOTO 30
80    END
```

```
RUN

INPUT ANY NUMBER
?-4
1.38629
```

INPUT ANY NUMBER
?16
2.77259
INPUT ANY NUMBER
?-2563
7.84893

END

Flowchart for ABS function example.

● **AND:** The AND statement is used in conjunction with the IF THEN statement. It allows the IF THEN statement to have two or more qualifiers instead of only one. The IF THEN statement is true if and only if both qualifiers are true.

EXAMPLE:

10   IF X = 10 AND Y = 15 THEN 600

In the above example both the first qualifier (X = 10) and the second (Y = 15) must be true if the branch to 600 is to occur.

PROGRAMMING EXAMPLE:

```
10    REM THIS PROGRAM DEMONSTRATES THE
20    REM AND STATEMENT
30    LET K = 10
```

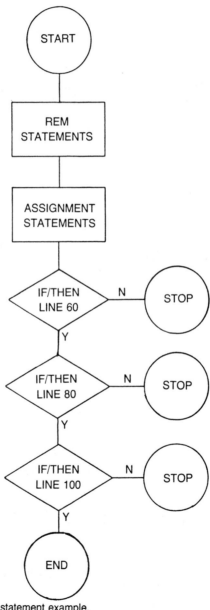

Flowchart for AND statement example.

```
40   LET J = 20
50   LET L = 30
60   IF K = J/2 AND L = K + J THEN 80
70   STOP
80   IF J = L − K AND J = K*2 THEN 100
90   STOP
100  IF K = 10 AND J = 20 AND L = 30 THEN 120
110  STOP
120  END
```

● **Argument:** An *argument* is any numeric or string quantity that is required by a mathematical or logical expression to operate on. The arguments of a function are those items that are used by that function to produce a result or evaluation of that function.

EXAMPLE:

1. SIN(X)
2. 2*3
3. A/B

In the above, X, 2, 3, A, and B are arguments of the function's sine, multiplication, and division, respectively.

● **Array:** A table or list of items is called an array. A list has only items that have a one-dimensional value, namely its position in the list relative to the first entry in the list. An array is a two-dimensional entity that has rows and columns; thus every item must have a row and a column value.

EXAMPLE:

```
LIST
3456.98
7856989
6756.09
6754444
```

The above list has 4 items. Each item may be identified by its position in the list, such as 6756.09 is the third item in the list.

45	78	67	78
53	67	98	23
32	84	21	90
34	29	53	71

The above is a table of numbers with four columns and four rows. Each item is identified by its row and column value. In the above example 84 is in the second row and the second column.

If the name of the above table was A then A(2,2) would stand for 84, the element in the second row and in the second column of the array named A.

● **ASC:** The ASC library function converts any single character to its ASCII equivalent. Thus this function will only accept a single character as an argument. One use of the ASC function is to permit alphabetization. As the code is in alphabetic sequence, we merely convert the characters to their ASCII values and compare them to find which is larger.

EXAMPLE:

```
10    LET A = ASC(Z)
20    LET B = ASC(P)
30    LET H = ASC(C)
40    LET J = ASC(K)
```

See *CHANGE* for table of ASCII codes.

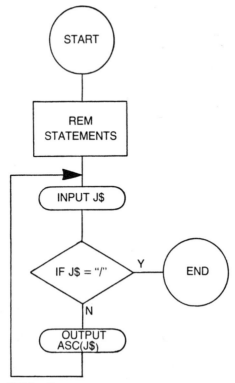

Flowchart for ASC function.

PROGRAMMING EXAMPLE:

```
10      REM THIS PROGRAM DEMONSTRATES
20      REM THE ASC FUNCTION
30      PRINT "INPUT A LETTER"
40      INPUT J$
50      IF J$ = "/" THEN 80
60      PRINT ASC (J$)
70      GOTO 30
80      END
```

RUN

INPUT A LETTER
?A
65
INPUT A LETTER
?K
75
INPUT A LETTER
?/

END

PROGRAMMING EXAMPLE:

```
10      REM THIS PROGRAM USES
20      REM THE ASC FUNCTION
30      PRINT "INPUT TWO LETTERS"
40      INPUT A$,B$
50      A = ASC(A$)
60      B = ASC(B$)
70      IF A>B THEN 110
80      IF A = B THEN 130
90      PRINT A$; "IS LESS THAN";B$
100     STOP
110     PRINT A$; "IS GREATER THAN";B$
120     STOP
130     PRINT A$; "IS EQUAL TO";B$
140     STOP
150     END
```

RUN
INPUT TWO LETTERS
?K,T
T IS GREATER THAN K

END

●**ASCII:** See *CHANGE*

●**Assignment:** The assignment statement assigns the value of a constant or a string to a variable. The value of the term on the right of the equal sign is assigned to the variable on the left.

EXAMPLES:

```
10    LET J = K−9
20    LET A2 = 365.25
30    LET Q$ = "HELLO"
40    LET K$ = J$
```
Similarly, we have
```
10    J = K−9
20    A2 = 365.25
30    Q$ = "HELLO" (Note: Strings must always be enclosed by
              quotation marks)
40    K$ = J$
```

The keyword LET is optional in some versions of BASIC.

An assignment statement does not correspond to an algebraic expression, for example:
```
10    J = J + 1
20    N = N*2
```
Assignment statements are always interpreted as carrying out the operations on the right and assigning the resulting value to the variable on the left. Thus the statement $J = J + 1$ is interpreted as, "Take the value of J, increment it by 1 and assign it to the variable J." Thereafter the variable J has a new value.

PROGRAMMING EXAMPLE:

```
10    REM THIS PROGRAM DEMONSTRATES THE
20    REM ASSIGNMENT STATEMENT
30    REM ASSIGNMENT USING LET
40    PRINT "INPUT A NUMBER THAT IS POSITIVE"
50    INPUT J
60    LET K = J*2
70    LET L = LOG(J)
80    LET M = SIN(J)
90    PRINT J,K,L,M
100   REM ASSIGNMENT NOT USING LET
```

```
110   K = J/2
120   L = J*LOG(J)
130   M = J/SIN(J)
140   PRINT J,K,L,M
150   END
```

Flowchart for Assignment statement.

●**ATN:** The library function ATN returns the arctangent of the argument enclosed in parentheses. The result is returned in radians on most computers.

EXAMPLES:
```
10    PRINT ATN(X)
20    Z = ATN(X)
```

PROGRAMMING EXAMPLE:
```
10    REM THIS PROGRAM DEMONSTRATES
20    REM THE ATN FUNCTION
30    PRINT "INPUT A NUMBER"
40    INPUT J
50    IF J = 0 THEN 80
60    PRINT ATN(J)
70    GOTO 30
80    END
```

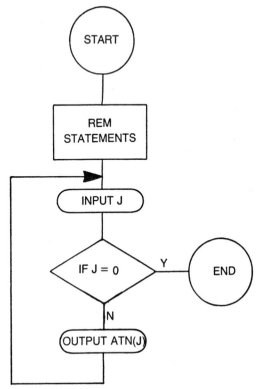

Flowchart for ATN function.

RUN

INPUT A NUMBER
?2
1.10715
INPUT A NUMBER
?3.14159
1.26263
INPUT A NUMBER
?1
0.78539
INPUT A NUMBER
?0

END

● **Back Slash:** See *Colon*.

● **BYE:** The BYE command, usually associated with large computer time-sharing system, returns the computer to the executive (operating system) mode.

● **CALL:** The purpose of the CALL function is to enable the program to produce results that can not be achieved by the language BASIC itself. The use of the CALL or USER statements allows the programmer to call upon a "machine language" subroutine. Most versions of BASIC require the programmer to reference the user-written code by addressing the first line of the subroutine by its actual absolute location in the computer's memory. In certain versions of BASIC the CALL statement can also be used to call a routine.

EXAMPLE:

MACHINE LANGUAGE
10   CALL 936 (where 936 is the absolute location in memory of the routine, 939 is in decimal notation.)
20   CALL C9A (Where C9A is the absolute location in memory of the routine, C9A is in hexadecimal notation.)
30   CALL "PLOT" (Where "PLOT" is the routine.)
    Using the CALL in conjunction with name subroutines, we can usually place variables after the routine name, separated by commas. These variables have assigned values which can be passed on to the routine as data.

EXAMPLE:

10   CALL "PLOT", A,B,C
20   CALL "CONTROL",K,J,L

Typical examples of the uses of the called machine language subroutines are control of floppy discs, tape drives, plotters, and externally controlled relays, switches, and other electronic equipment.

PROGRAMMING EXAMPLE:

10   REM THIS PROGRAM DEMONSTRATES THE
20   REM CALL OR USER FUNCTION.
30   CALL 936
40   LET N = 14
50   LET J = N*N
60   LET K = 18
70   CALL 1404
80   LET K = K − 1
90   IF K > = 10 THEN 70
100   END

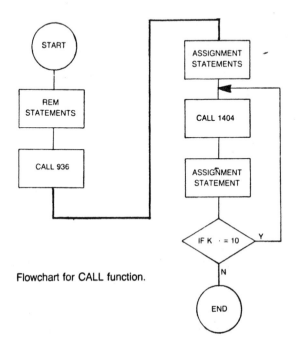

Flowchart for CALL function.

● **CATALOG:** See *CAT*.

● **CAT:** The CATALOG or CAT command allows the user to view the list of names of all programs previously saved by the user.

● **CHANGE:** When a computer stores the characters of a string, it does not store the characters directly, but as an encoded sequence of numbers.

Several different numerical coding schemes can be used, but the most common is the 7-bit ASCII code. The following table shows the ASCII (American Standard Code for Information Interchange) coding.

CHARACTER	CODE	CHARACTER	CODE
A	65	2	50
B	66	3	51
C	67	4	52
D	68	5	53
E	69	6	54
F	70	7	55
G	71	8	56
H	72	9	57
I	73	+	43
J	74	−	45
K	75	/	47
L	76	*	42
M	77	↑	94
N	78	(	40
O	79	)	41
P	80	<	60
Q	81	>	62
R	82	=	61
S	83	?	63
T	84	$	36
U	85	"	34
V	86	'	44
W	87	.	46
X	88	;	59
Y	89	CARRIAGE	
Z	90	RETURN (CR)	13
0	48	LINE FEED (LF)	10
1	49	SPACE	32

The computer automatically carries out the conversion from characters to numbers and the reverse. The operation is generally *transparent*; that is, the user is not usually even aware of the fact that the computer is encoding the characters.

Sometimes it is necessary to use the numeric equivalent of the character in a string. This has the advantage of allowing the user to manipulate each character individually. This conversion is carried out by the CHANGE statement.

The CHANGE statement may be written in two different ways.

METHOD 1:

The keyword CHANGE, is followed by a string variable, the keyword TO and a numeric list. The items in this statement must be kept in that order.

This statement causes each character in the string to be converted to its numerical equivalent and stored in a numeric list.

The first element in the numeric list (that is the element with a subscript of zero) will indicate the number of encoded characters contained in the list.

EXAMPLE:

```
10    LET J$ = "JANE"
20    . . . . . . . . . .
30    CHANGE J$ TO K
```

In the previous example the elements of K will be the following.

$K(0) = 4$
$K(1) = 74$
$K(2) = 65$
$K(3) = 78$
$K(4) = 69$

METHOD 2:

The string variable and the numeric list may be interchanged.

```
10    LET J(0) = 3
20    LET J(1) = 75
30    LET J(2) = 69
40    LET J(3) = 78
50    CHANGE J TO K$
```

In the example just shown, K$ will be assigned the string KEN.

PROGRAMMING EXAMPLE:

```
10    REM THIS PROGRAM DEMONSTRATES
20    REM THE CHANGE STATEMENT
```

30   CHANGE

```
30      PRINT "INPUT A WORD"
40      INPUT J$
50      CHANGE J$ TO K
60      FOR I = 0 TO LEN(J$)
70      PRINT K(I),
80      NEXT I
90      PRINT
100     PRINT "WE WILL NOW CHANGE NUMBERS TO A
        STRING"
110     PRINT "HOW MANY NUMBERS"
120     INPUT L
130     LET X(O) = L
140     FOR M = 1 TO L
150     PRINT "INPUT A NUMBER"
160     INPUT L
170     LET X(M) = L
180     NEXT M
190     CHANGE X TO J$
200     PRINT J$
210     END
```

RUN

```
INPUT A WORD
?JAYN
4    74    65    89    78
WE WILL NOW CHANGE NUMBERS TO A STRING
HOW MANY NUMBERS
?3
INPUT A NUMBER
?75
INPUT A NUMBER
?69
INPUT A NUMBER
?78
KEN
```

END

Flowchart for CHANGE statement.

●**CHR$:** The library function CHR$ is the opposite of the library function ASC. The CHR$ function converts an ASCII code into a character. Obviously the argument must be a recognized ASCII integer quantity. All non-integer values will be truncated.

EXAMPLE:

```
10    LET Z$ = CHR$(X)
20    LET K$ = CHR$(65)
30    LET H$ = CHR$(74)
40    LET K$ = CHR$(75)
```

PROGRAMMING EXAMPLE:

```
10    REM THIS PROGRAM DEMONSTRATES
20    REM THE CHR$ FUNCTION
30    PRINT "INPUT A NUMBER"
40    INPUT K
50    LET J$ = CHR$(K)
60    PRINT J$
70    GOTO 30
80    END
```

RUN

```
INPUT A NUMBER
?80
P
INPUT A NUMBER
?63
?
INPUT A NUMBER
?50
Z
INPUT A NUMBER
?74
J
```

END

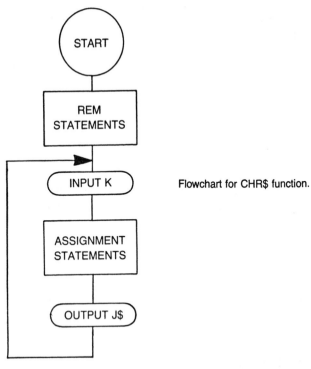

Flowchart for CHR$ function.

● **CLEAR:** In some versions of BASIC the command CLEAR zeroes all variables and strings. In other versions the CLEAR command clears or erases the current program in memory.

● **Colon(:):**The colon is used in BASIC to allow more than one statement to be included in one line number. Depending on the version of BASIC used either the colon (:), slash (/) or back slash (\) is used between different statements. The advantage of using multiple statements per line is that memory is saved by not having to specify as many line numbers.

EXAMPLE:

```
10    LET K =J/LET H = Z*2/LET P = LET P = 3.1415
20    PRINT:PRINT:PRINT "ENTER VALUE":INPUT K
```

The above may also be written as:

```
10    LET K = J: LET H =Z*2/LET P = 3.1415
or
20    PRINT\PRINT\PRINT "ENTER VALUE"\INPUT K
```

Depending on the version of BASIC caution must be exercised with conditional statements. Some versions fall through to the next statement in a multi-statement line, while others fall through to the next line number.

EXAMPLE:

```
10    IF X = Y THEN PRINT Y : GOTO 100
20    PRINT X
```

If the condition X = Y is true Y should be printed and the execution transferred to line 100. If the condition is not met, transfer should be given to line 100.

If the version of BASIC used had "fall through" to the next line, the true condition would work as above, but in the false condition transfer would go to line 20, not line 100. This occurs because after the conditional test is made and is found false, transfer goes to the next line, not to the next statement.

Also depending on the version being used, more than one line of code may be written under one line number. (Usually a fixed maximum of characters is set, typically around 255 for the number of characters in a multi-statement.)

EXAMPLE:

```
10    LET K = J: FOR I = 1 TO 20: PRINT I:
      PRINT: PRINT K*I: NEXT I
20    PRINT: PRINT "LOOP FINISHED": END
```

● **Concatenation:** Concatenation is the process of adding two or more strings together, such as "HELLO" and "JANE", to form one string, "HELLO JANE". In concatenation we use the + (plus) symbol and form an assignment statement using strings and/or string variables.

EXAMPLE:

```
10    LET K$ = J$ + L$
20    LET S$ = "MICE" + " " + "ARE" + " " + "NICE"
30    LET Z$ = "VALVE" + L$
40    LET H$ = Q$ + "ATOMS"
50    LET P$ = B$ + "ARE" + C$
```

Note: If spaces are required, they must either be part of the string or variable, or be concatenated separately as line 20 of the above example.

PROGRAMMING EXAMPLE:

```
10     REM THIS PROGRAM DEMONSTRATES
20     REM THE CONCATENATION FUNCTION
30     PRINT "ENTER ANY THREE WORDS"
40     INPUT J$,K$,L$
50     LET A$ = " "
60     LET B$ = J$ + A$ + K$ + A$ + L$
70     PRINT B$
80     IF B$ = "STOP NOW OK" THEN 100
90     GOTO 30
100    END
```

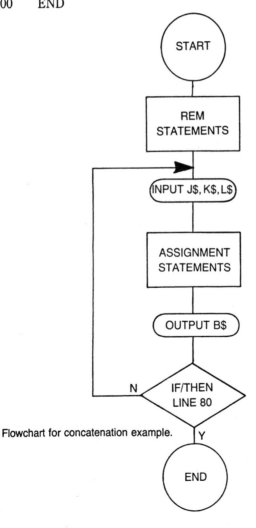

Flowchart for concatenation example.

RUN

ENTER ANY THREE WORDS
?MICE,ARE,NICE
MICE ARE NICE
ENTER ANY THREE WORDS
?THIS,IS,BASIC
THIS IS BASIC
ENTER ANY THREE WORDS
?STOP,NOW,OK
STOP NOW OK

END

●**Conditional Branching:** The IF–THEN statement is the basis of the conditional branching operation in BASIC. This statement consists of the key words IF and THEN, separated by a relation, and followed by the number of the line to be branched to. Note: In some versions of BASIC it is allowable to place an AS-SIGNMENT or other statement after the THEN required.

EXAMPLE:

```
10    IF J = K THEN 100
20    IF X < > 10 THEN 120
30    IF J1 < 2 THEN 100
40    IF Q > 37 THEN 150
50    IF H > = 86 THEN 200
60    IF A < = 10 THEN 80
```

If the condition is satisfied, the branch will occur; otherwise, the next line will be executed.

For an IF THEN statement that transfers control to another line, some versions of BASIC allow the use of the word GOTO instead of THEN.

EXAMPLE:

```
10    IF J = K GOTO 100
```

Conditional branching is used with strings as well as with numerics. In the case of a string as opposed to a string variable (i.e., A$), the string must be enclosed in quotation marks.

EXAMPLE:

```
10    IF K$ = "KEN" THEN 100
20    IF K$ = J$ THEN 500
```

PROGRAMMING EXAMPLE:

```
10    REM THIS PROGRAM DEMONSTRATES
20    REM THE IF-THEN STATEMENT
30    INPUT J
40    IF J = 0 THEN 70
50    PRINT "J IS NON-ZERO"
60    GOTO 30
70    PRINT "J IS ZERO"
80    GOTO 30
90    END
```

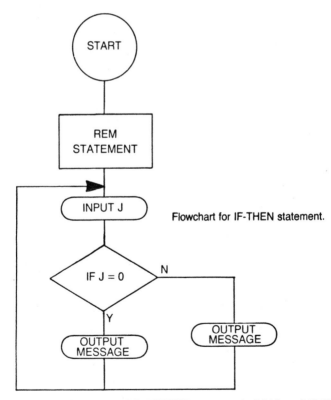

Flowchart for IF-THEN statement.

●**CONTINUE:** The CONTINUE command (CON or CONT in some versions of BASIC) restarts program execution after a CONTROL-C is typed.

● **Control Characters:** Control characters are generated by holding down the CTRL key while typing the specified letter. Generally the control character is not printed.

The following is a list of control characters. Remember to hold down the CTRL key while typing the letter specified!

C . . . . . Halts a program
G . . . . . Sounds bell
H . . . . . Backspaces cursor
J . . . . . Issues line feed
V . . . . . Forward spaces cursor
X . . . . . Deletes current line

● **COPY:** Different versions of BASIC have different methods of controlling peripheral devices. The COPY command is usually used with a computer having both a video terminal (CRT) and a printer.

After typing in the keyword or command COPY the computer will utilize the printer to make a " hard copy " of what is presently on the CRT screen.

● **COS:** The library function COS returns the cosine of the argument in parentheses. The argument is generally interpreted as being in radians.

EXAMPLES:

```
10    PRINT COS(Y)
20    K = COS(J)
```

PROGRAMMING EXAMPLE:

```
10    REM THIS PROGRAM DEMONSTRATES
20    REM THE COS FUNCTION
30    PRINT "INPUT A NUMBER"
40    INPUT J
50    IF J = 0 THEN 80
60    PRINT COS(J)
70    GOTO 30
80    END
```

RUN

INPUT A NUMBER
?3.14159
− 1
INPUT A NUMBER
?1.2
0.36235
INPUT A NUMBER
?6.28319
1
INPUT A NUMBER
?0

END

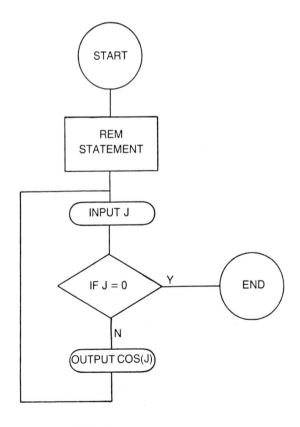

Flowchart for COS function.

●**DEF:** When a program section is used as a function, and is used quite often during the main program, the programmer can use the DEF statement.

DEF allows the user to write a function such as A = (A − 3)/A and use it repeatedly throughout the program by calling the function.

The DEF statement consists of the keyword DEF and the function definition. The function definition is the function name followed by an equal sign, followed by the appropriate variable, constant, or formula. Both numeric and string functions can be defined by the DEF statement. If the function requires arguments then they must appear directly after the function name, enclosed in parentheses and separated by commas.

If the function is numeric, the function name must consist of three letters, the first two of which being FN. Thus any given program may have 26 different numeric functions ranging from FNA to FNZ. We may also have 26 different string functions labeled FNA$ to FNZ$. Numeric and string functions having the same first three letters, such as FNJ and FNJ$, are considered to be different functions. Thus any program may contain 52 functions. As can be seen, the string function name must end in a dollar sign.

EXAMPLE:

```
10    DEF FNJ(K,L) = (K − 2)/(L − 3)
20    DEF FNK$ = "EMPLOYEE STATUS"
30    DEF FNZ(X,Y) = (X − Y) − (Y − X)
```

A DEF statement may appear anywhere within the BASIC program. However it is considered good practice to group all the DEF statements together and place them near the beginning or end of the program.

It should be obvious that the DEF statement only defines a function but does not evaluate it.

PROGRAMMING EXAMPLE:

```
10    REM THIS PROGRAM DEMONSTRATES
20    REM THE DEF STATEMENT
30    DEF FNA(X) = LOG(X)/X
40    DEF FNB(X) = SIN(X)/K
50    DEF FNC(X) = COS(X)/L
60    PRINT "INPUT A NUMBER"
70    INPUT J
80    LET J = ABS(J)
```

```
90      LET K = 10
100     LET L = 20
110     LET M = FNA(J)
120     LET N = FNB(J)
130     LET P = FNC(J)
140     PRINT M,N,P
150     END
```

RUN

```
INPUT A NUMBER
?8
0.25993      0.09894      -0.00728
```

END

    In the above example we can see another property of the DEF statement. Any variables (K,L) not included in parentheses (non-defined arguments) in the DEF statement name will be used as having the most recent values assigned to them.

Flowchart for DEF statement.

Flowchart for DET function.

●**DET:** Once we determine the inverse of a square matrix we may further determine its determinant by using the library function DET. The DET function returns a single numeric value and requires no argument. One obvious use of the DET statement is to determine if a given matrix does have an inverse. If the inverse does not exist, the determinant will be zero.

Note: The DET library function may only be referenced after a MAT INV statement. If the DET function returns a zero for a given matrix, the inverse determined by the preceding MAT INV statement will not be meaningful.

EXAMPLE:

```
10    MAT J = INV(K)
20    PRINT DET
```

PROGRAMMING EXAMPLE:

```
10    REM THIS PROGRAM DEMONSTRATES
20    REM THE DET FUNCTION
30    DIM J(5,5),K(5,5),L(5,5)
40    MAT READ J
50    MAT K = INV(J)
60    PRINT DET
70    DATA 6,8,9,4,1,2,4,6,2,4,8,9,2,1,3
80    DATA 7,3,2,1,4,6,5,3,1,4
90    END
```

●**DIM:** Some versions of BASIC assign 121 elements (11 columns, 11 rows) to every table and 11 elements to every list. Thus each subscript can generally range from 0 to 10 (occasionally 1 to 11). In versions of BASIC which do not automatically assign elements to lists and tables, or if you desire more than 11 elements to a list or 11 rows by 11 columns to a table, you must use the DIMENSION (DIM) statement.

The DIM statement consists of the keyword DIM followed by various array names, separated by commas. Each and every array name must be followed by at least one number (for lists) or two numbers separated by a comma for tables. In either case, the numeric values are placed in parentheses directly following the array name.

EXAMPLE:

```
10    DIM J(19), K(28), L(4), M(8,10)
20    DIM A(10,20), B(250), X(65), J$(35)
30    DIM F(9), K$(14,14), J$(9,10)
```

A DIM statement can occur anywhere in a BASIC program but it is considered good practice to place all DIM statements at the very beginning.

PROGRAMMING EXAMPLE:

```
10    REM THIS PROGRAM DEMONSTRATES THE
20    REM DIM STATEMENT
30    DIM A$(20),B$(3),C(60)
40    FOR I = 1 TO 60
50    LET C(I) = I
60    NEXT I
70    END
```

Flowchart for DIM statement.

● **DIMENSION:** See *DIM*.

● **DO END:** See *IF-THEN DO, ELSE*

● **Dummy Arguments:** Whenever a certain function requires an argument in advance, such as the DEF statement, the actual value of the argument is not required. What is required is the number and type of arguments being used. An argument that only expresses location, type and use is called a *dummy argument*. A dummy argument "tells" the function in advance that a numeric or string will be used later on and how many "real" arguments are to be evaluated. See *DEF*.

● **ELSE:** See *IF-THEN DO, ELSE*

● **END:** The END statement indicates the end of the program. When the computer reads this statement it interprets it to mean stop execution.

   In most versions of BASIC this must be the last statement in the program. Therefore, it must be preceded by the highest line number.

EXAMPLE:

999   END

● **EXP:** The library function EXP raises the constant *e* (2.71828) to the power X (*e***X).

EXAMPLES:

10   PRINT EXP(J)
20   Z = EXP(Q)

PROGRAMMING EXAMPLE:

```
10    REM THIS PROGRAM DEMONSTRATES
20    REM THE EXP FUNCTION
30    PRINT "INPUT A NUMBER FROM 1 TO 10"
40    INPUT J
50    FOR I = 1 TO J
60    PRINT EXP(I)
70    NEXT I
80    END
```

RUN

INPUT A NUMBER FROM 1 TO 10
?6
2.71828
7.38906
20.0855
54.5981
148.413
403.429

END

Flowchart for EXP function.

● **Files:** A *file* consists of a group of records, where each record may be considered to be a group of variables.

To use a filing cabinet for comparison, a variable is a line of printing, a number, or a slip. A record is a file folder. The whole drawer, or cabinet, or aisle of cabinets, is the file.

Files usually contain related data, but this is the programmer's decision.

As every version of BASIC has its own way of defining files and file handling, it is always best to consult the user's manual for the computer being used. See also *Sequential Data Files* and *Random Data Files*.

● **FN:** To reference a function predefined by a DEF statement, a typical assignment statement is written with the function name acting as though it were a library function, with the function name followed in parentheses by an argument.

When a function is evaluated, the values of the arguments are specified by the function reference and not by the function definition. For this reason any arguments appearing with a DEF statement are called *dummy arguments*. The arguments in the reference need not be the same as those appearing in the definition, but they must be of the same type (i.e., numeric or string) and number. See *Dummy Arguments*.

EXAMPLE:

```
10    DEF FNK(J) = (J − 3)/J
20    .........
30    .........
40    LET H = FNK(Z) −100
50    .........
60    .........
70    IF FNK(P) = 110 THEN 100
80    PRINT FNK(A)
90    STOP
100   PRINT "SOLUTION IS";P
110   END
```

The arguments in the reference must have a one-to-one correspondence with the dummy arguments when two or more arguments are used. The correspondence is not by name, but by type and number or arguments.

Dummy arguments must be non-subscripted variables, but the arguments present in the function reference may be written as constants, subscripted variables, formulae or even other references.

PROGRAMMING EXAMPLE:

```
10    REM THIS PROGRAM DEMONSTRATES
20    REM THE FN STATEMENT
30    DEF FNA(X) = LOG(X)*2
40    FOR I = 1 TO 10
50    PRINT FNA(I)
60    NEXT I
70    END
```

RUN

```
0
1.38628
2.19722
2.77258
3.21886
3.58352
3.89182
4.15888
4.39444
4.60516
```

END

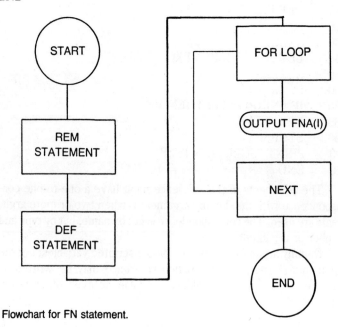

Flowchart for FN statement.

● **FOR-TO:** In BASIC, if we know how many times a loop should be performed we use the FOR-TO statement, which specifies how many times the loop is to be executed. Directly following the keyword FOR is the running variable, which must be a non-subscripted numeric variable, whose value changes each time the loop is executed. The number of times the loop is executed is specified by the initial and final values of the running variable.

EXAMPLE:

```
10    FOR J = 1 TO 50
20    FOR K = 10 TO 100
30    FOR L = 7 TO 10
```

If we set up a FOR-TO statement such as,

$$FOR\ I = 1\ TO\ 10$$

the following occurs. Each time the loop is run, I is initially set to 1. I is then incremented by 1 each time the loop is repeated, until I has reached the final value of 10.

The running variable will always be incremented by 1 unless a contrary statement is included. The STEP statement changes the value by which I changes. Using the STEP statement, we may increment or decrement the running variable. In most versions of BASIC we can also use variables or formulae for the initial and final values of the running variable and the step size.

EXAMPLE:

```
10    FOR J = K TO X STEP Z
20    FOR K = 1 TO Q STEP -Z
30    FOR J = K/L TO M+ L STEP K-1
```

Some versions of BASIC allow the interchange of the keywords STEP and BY. Thus we can have:

$$FOR\ K = J\ TO\ M\ BY\ L$$

To close the FOR-TO loop we use the keyword NEXT. All FOR-TO loops must end in a NEXT statement. The NEXT statement consists of a statement number (line number) and the keyword NEXT, followed by the running variable name. Of course the running variable must be the running variable used in the corresponding FOR-TO statement.

EXAMPLE:

```
10     FOR K = J TO M
20     ..........
30     ..........
40     ..........
50     ..........
60     NEXT K
```

The following rules always apply in the FOR-TO-STEP loop:

1) The running variable may appear in a statement within the loop, but its value must and cannot be changed or altered.

2) If the final and initial values of the running variable are equal and the step size is nonzero, the loop will be executed once.

3) The loop will not be executed under the following conditions:

   A) The final and intial running variable values are equal and the step size is zero.

   B) The final value is less than the initial value and the step size is positive.

   C) The final value is greater than the initial value and the step size is negative.

4) Control can be transferred out of a loop but not into one.

PROGRAMMING EXAMPLE:

```
10     REM THIS PROGRAM DEMONSTRATES
20     REM THE FOR-TO STATEMENT
30     FOR I = 1 TO 10
40     PRINT I*10
50     NEXT I
60     END
```

RUN

```
10
20
30
40
50
60
70
80
```

90
100

END

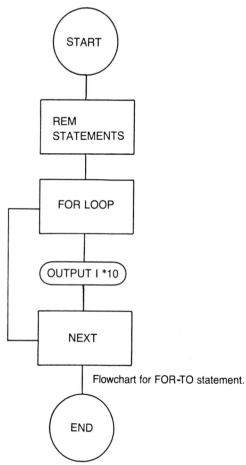

Flowchart for FOR-TO statement.

● **FRE:** The FRE statement requires either a zero as an argument, which returns the number of memory bytes currently unused by BASIC not including strings,

EXAMPLE:

10   PRINT FRE(0)

or A$ as an argument which returns the number of unused memory bytes including strings.

EXAMPLE:

10   PRINT FRE(A$)

●**GOSUB:** A subroutine is referenced by the keyword GOSUB followed by the line number of the first statement in the subroutine structure. When the computer executes this instruction, control is transferred to the line indicated by the GOSUB statement; but the computer "remembers" the line in the program where the sub-routine call was generated. On encountering a RETURN statement, the computer returns control to the statement following the one that was kept in memory. That is, control is transferred to the statement immediately following the subroutine call.

EXAMPLE:

```
10     LET J = 25
20     LET K = 2
30     GOSUB 60
40     PRINT L
50     ..........
60     LET L = J/K
70     RETURN
```

Note: Unless the statement prior to the first statement of the subroutine is a branch or a STOP statement, the subroutine will be executed as part of the main program.

A program may contain more than one reference to the same subroutine procedure. Control will always be returned to the statement following the point of call.

EXAMPLE:

```
10     LET A = 10
20     LET B = 2
30     GOSUB 100
40     PRINT C
50     GOSUB 100
60     PRINT C-2
70     ..........
80     ..........
90     ..........
100     LET C = A/B
110     RETURN
```

A subroutine itself may call a subroutine. This is called *nesting* (see *Nested Loops*). The number of levels in the nest is determined by the version of BASIC used. The following rule always applies with nested subroutines: if Subroutine X calls Subroutine Z, then Subroutine Z must not call Subroutine X.

PROGRAMMING EXAMPLE:

```
10   REM THIS PROGRAM DEMONSTRATES
20   REM THE GOSUB STATEMENT
30   PRINT "ENTER A NUMBER"
40   INPUT J
50   IF J = 0 THEN 110
```

Flowchart for GOSUB statement.

```
60      GOSUB 90
70      PRINT K
80      GOTO 30
90      LET K = (J*2)/3
100     RETURN
110     END
```

RUN

ENTER A NUMBER
?5
3.33333
ENTER A NUMBER
?1256
837.333
ENTER A NUMBER
?31.3
20.8666
ENTER A NUMBER
?0

END

● **GOTO:** In a BASIC program the flow of execution is from the smallest line number to the largest line number. If an *unconditional* jump is required, a jump that requires no logic to see if it is to be performed or not, a GOTO statement is used. The GOTO statement or unconditional jump is usually referred to as an *unconditional branch statement*. The GOTO statement can transfer control to any other statement with the program. Once the branch is completed, execution flow continues from smallest to largest line number.

EXAMPLE:

```
10      GOTO 100
20      GOTO 1090
```

It should be noted that depending on the version of BASIC used GOTO may be one word, two words or either.

PROGRAMMING EXAMPLE:

```
10      REM THIS PROGRAM DEMONSTRATES CONDI-
        TIONAL
```

```
20      REM BRANCHING OUT OF A GOTO LOOP
30      REM THIS PROGRAM COMPUTES THE AVERAGE
40      REM OF N NUMBERS
50      REM TO EXIT THE LOOP TYPE A 0
60      LET K = 0
70      LET N = 0
80      INPUT J
90      IF J = 0 THEN 130
100     LET K = K + J
110     LET N = N + 1
120     GOTO 80
130     PRINT "SUM = ";K
140     PRINT "AVERAGE = ";K/N
150     END
```

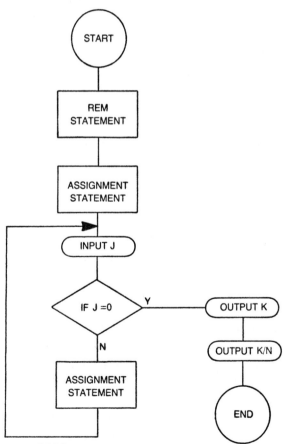

Flowchart for GOTO Loop.

●**Graphical Output:** The numeric lists or tables produced by computer programs are often plotted by hand on graph paper, but it is very useful if the computer can produce graphical output without special equipment. CRT video terminal is not usually a good choice because the resolution of graph depends upon the number of horizontal and vertical positions available. Although both the CRT and typical printers have the same number of horizontal positions, the printer can produce literally infinite vertical positions, if we view the length as vertical. Alternatively, the paper's width could be viewed as vertical and thus we can have an extended horizontal graph.

The easiest method for producing a graph is to use a FOR-TO loop which has a PRINT statement containing the TAB function within the structure.

The following are typical routines that may be used in production of graphs.

X AXIS (axis across the width of the paper)

```
10    FOR J = 0 TO 71
20    PRINT TAB(J);".";
30    NEXT J
```

Y AXIS (along the length of the paper)
Since we are plotting the graph along the length of the paper, we must plot the Y axis (length axis) at the same time.

```
10    FOR B = Y TO Z
20    ..........
30    ..........
40    PRINT "."; TAB(A);"*"
50    ..........
60    ..........
70    NEXT X
```

Line 40 prints both the Y axis and also the graph, in this case composed of asterisks (*). Lines 20, 30, 50, and 60 generate the values for A. Obviously A is being plotted against B; as each cycle of the loop moves along the Y axis the TAB function places the * in the proper position as determined by the formula generating the value of A.

●**Hierarchy:** When two or more operators are used in the same linear formula, questions in meanings may arise. Consider the case of 28*K−19*J. Does this correspond to the algebraic term (28K)—

(19J) or to 28(K−19J)? Also consider K/J*4,is this K/(4J) or 4(K/J). These problems are taken care of by the following hierarchy of operations:

1) All exponentiation operations are performed first.
2) Multiplication and division are carried out after exponentiation. Multiplication and division have no hierarchy over each other; one will not necessarily precede the other.
3) Addition and subtraction are always the last to be carried out. Here also no hierarchy exists between the two.

Within any given hierachical group, the operations are carried out from left to right.

Parentheses change the order of normal hierachical flow in a formula. See *Parentheses*.

●**HOME:** The HOME command instructs the computer to return the display cursor to the "home" position, which is usually either the upper left or lower left corner of the CRT screen. Some versions of BASIC use a CALL or USER statement to achieve the same results.

●**IF-END:** See *Sequential Data Files Reading or Writing*.

●**IF-THEN:** See *Conditional Branching*.

●**IF-THEN DO,ELSE:** The IF-THEN DO,ELSE statement occurs in certain versions of BASIC and allows the user to write a complete procedure in the lines between the IF-THEN DO and the ELSE. Following the ELSE statement the user may also write a complete procedure. The line following the procedure after the ELSE and after the DO must contain only the keyword DOEND (DO END).

The format is therefore the following:

```
10    IF(EXPRESSION) THEN DO
20    ............procedure.....................
30    ........................................
40    DO END
50    ELSE (EXPRESSION OR STATEMENT)
60    DO END
```

●**INPUT:** The input statement is used to enter numeric or string data into the computer during program execution. This statement consists of the keyword INPUT, followed by the list of variables separated by commas. Both numeric and string variables may be included in one INPUT statement.

EXAMPLE:

```
10      INPUT K,J
20      INPUT K$, J$, S$
30      INPUT K1$, J, S3$
```

During program execution, a question mark (?) is sent to the output device when an INPUT statement is encountered. The question mark is usually placed on a new line unless a PRINT statement previous to it included a semi-colon as its last character.

An INPUT statement may also be combined with a PRINT statement as follows:

EXAMPLE:

INPUT "HOW OLD ARE YOU", J

In this case the computer will print the string HOW OLD ARE YOU on a new line, immediately follow it with a question mark and wait for the input data.

In either case, when the INPUT statement is encountered and the question mark has been printed, the computer will suspend program execution until the data has been entered. After the data has been entered, the user must hit the return key to tell the computer that the data has been entered and that it can continue execution.

The following rules must be adhered to when using the INPUT statement:

1) The data entered must correspond to the variables listed in the INPUT statement.
2) The data entered, if it is more than one item, must be separated by commas.
3) A string that contains a comma, or begins with a blank space, or ends in a blank space, must be placed in quotation marks.

The INPUT statement is used for the conversation mode of BASIC and when large quantities of data are not required. If large volumes of data are required, the READ, DATA statements should be used.

PROGRAMMING EXAMPLE:

```
10      REM THIS PROGRAM DEMONSTRATES THE
20      REM INPUT STATEMENT
```

```
30      INPUT X
40      LET R = (X/3.14159)**.5
50      PRINT "RADIUS = ";R
60      INPUT B,H
70      LET A = (B*H)/2
80      PRINT "AREA = ";A
90      INPUT K,J,L,M,N,O,P
100     LET S = K + J + L + M + N + O + P
110     PRINT "SUM = ";S
120     END
```

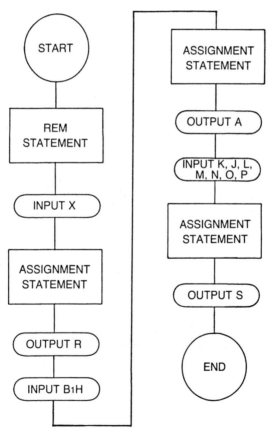

Flowchart for INPUT statement.

●**INSTR:** This function searches for a second string within the first string. The keyword INSTR is followed in parentheses by a numeric formula, and the two string formulae.

To illustrate:

10   INSTR (X, Y, Z)

X is a numeric formula (constant or variable) truncated to an integer and indicates the starting position of the search. If X is not present, the first character of the string to be searched is the starting position by default. Y is the string being sought for, and Z is the string being searched.

INSTR returns the position of the first character in the substring if found, 0 if not.

EXAMPLE:

10   INSTR(10, J$, K$)
20   INSTR(C, "A", J$)
30   INSTR("BYE", "GOODBYE")

Flowchart for INSTR function.

PROGRAMMING EXAMPLE:

```
10    REM THIS PROGRAM DEMONSTRATES
20    REM THE INSTR FUNCTION
30    PRINT "ENTER TWO WORDS, THE FIRST MUST"
40    PRINT "BE CONTAINED IN THE SECOND"
50    INPUT J$,K$
60    LET X = INSTR(J$,K$)
70    PRINT X
80    END
```

RUN

```
ENTER TWO WORDS, THE FIRST MUST
BE CONTAINED IN THE SECOND
?BYE,GOODBYE
5
```

END

● **INT:** The library function INT returns the largest integer less than or equal to the argument enclosed in parentheses.

EXAMPLE:

```
10    PRINT INT(Q)
20    Z = INT(X + Y)
```

PROGRAMMING EXAMPLE:

```
10    REM THIS PROGRAM DEMONSTRATES
20    REM THE INT FUNCTION
30    FOR I = 1 TO 10
40    LET J = I/3
50    PRINT INT(J)
60    NEXT I
70    END
```

RUN

```
0
0
1
1
```

62   INT

1
2
2
2
3
3

END

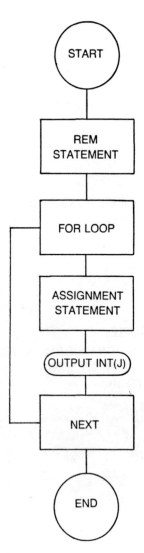

Flowchart for INT function.

● **LEFT$:** The library function LEFT$ returns the leftmost N characters of a string expression X$. Usually in BASIC N must be greater than or equal to zero and less than 255.

EXAMPLE:

```
10    PRINT LEFT$(X$,N)
20    PRINT LEFT$(J$,10)
```

PROGRAMMING EXAMPLE:

```
10    REM THIS PROGRAM DEMONSTRATES
20    REM THE LEFT$ FUNCTION
30    INPUT J$
40    FOR N = 1 TO LEN(J$)
50    PRINT LEFT$(J$,N)
60    NEXT N
70    END
```

RUN

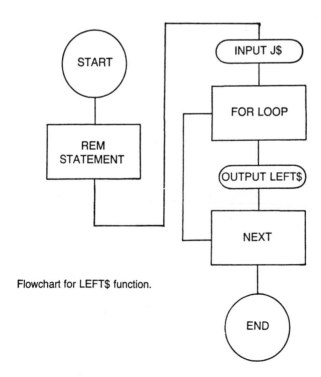

Flowchart for LEFT$ function.

```
?A BASIC PROGRAM
A
A
A B
A BA
A BAS
A BASI
A BASIC
A BASIC
A BASIC P
A BASIC PR
A BASIC PRO
A BASIC PROG
A BASIC PROGR
A BASIC PROGRA
A BASIC PROGRAM

END
```

●**LEN:** The LEN library function computes the number of characters in a string. It is written as LEN followed by the string in parentheses. Some versions require the string to be also enclosed in quotation marks unless the variable is reference only.

EXAMPLE:

```
10     K = LEN("HOUSE")
20     H = LEN(A$)
30     J = LEN("JANE")
```

In the last example (line 30) J will be assigned the value 4.

PROGRAMMING EXAMPLE:

```
10     REM THIS PROGRAM DEMONSTRATES
20     REM THE LEN FUNCTION
30     PRINT "ENTER A STRING"
40     INPUT J$
50     IF J$ = "END" THEN 80
60     PRINT LEN(J$)
70     GOTO 30
80     END
```

RUN

ENTER A STRING
? HELLO
5
ENTER A STRING
?MICE ARE NICE
13
ENTER A STRING
?BASIC LANGUAGE IS EASY
21
ENTER A STRING
?END

END

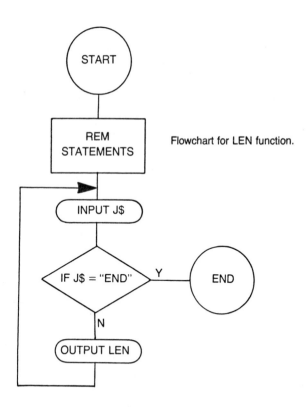

Flowchart for LEN function.

●**LENGTH:** LENGTH is generally a BASIC command, not a statement. It is used to ascertain the length of the current program residing in memory. When the user types in LENGTH during command mode, the total number of characters will be displayed.

●**LET:** See *Assignment*.

●**Library Functions:** The library functions, often called elementary or standard functions, provide a quick and easy method of evaluating mathematical operations, and, in some versions of BASIC, logical operations.

The library functions are prewritten routines that are included as an integral part of the BASIC language. By using the library functions, the user can avoid writing an explicit routine to achieve the same end.

Each function is accessed by stating its name and supplying the required information the function needs. Typically the required information is presented within parentheses. This information which is given to the library function is called an argument of the function.

The following is a table of typical library functions:

FUNCTION	USAGE	DESCRIPTION
ABS	Y = ABS(X)	CALCULATE ABSOLUTE VALUE
ATN	Y = ATN(X)	CALCULATE ARCTANGENT
COS	Y = COS(X)	CALCULATE COSINE
COT	Y = COT(X)	CALCULATE COTANGENT
EXP	Y = EXP(X)	RAISE E TO THE X POWER
INT	Y = INT(X)	CALCULATE LARGEST INTEGER NOT EXCEEDING X
LOG	Y = LOG(X)	CALCULATES NATURAL LOG
SGN	Y = SGN(X)	DETERMINES THE SIGN
SIN	Y = SIN(X)	CALCULATES THE SINE
SQR	Y = SQR(X)	CALCULATES THE SQUARE ROOT
TAB	PRINT TAB(N)X	STARTS PRINTING AT A GIVEN COLUMN
TAN	Y = TAN(X)	CALCULATES TANGENT

In most versions of BASIC the trigonometric library functions use the radian system as opposed to degrees. Of course, as with conventional mathematics, the rules governing trig functions and logs still apply.

●**Line Numbers:** Every BASIC program demands that each line of code be preceded by a line number. Some versions of BASIC allow more than one statement per line and more than one line of code per line number.

It is a good idea to write the program starting at line 10 and incrementing by 10 for each line number to allow for inserts.

The BASIC language will automatically insert new lines of code according to their line numbers. If the line number used for the insert already exists, the old line will be replaced by the new.

Except for branching deliberately introduced by the programmer, BASIC is always executed from smallest to largest line numbers.

●**LIST:** The LIST command displays the program starting from the smallest line number and ascending to the largest. The LIST command comes in a few different "varieties":

LIST: . . . . . Lists the total program.

LIST X: . . . . Lists line X if it exists.

LIST X-: . . . . Lists all line numbers in a program with a line number equal to or greater than X.

LIST-X: . . . . Lists all line numbers in a program equal to or less than X.

LIST X-Y: . . . Lists all line numbers in a program from X to Y.

LIST X,Y: . . . Same as LIST X-Y.

●**Lists and Tables:** When writing a complex or even a not-so-complex program it is often convenient and useful to be able to refer to an entire collection of data at one time. A collection of data in BASIC is called an *array*. We can have a one dimensional array, usually called a list, and we can have a two-dimensional array, the table. Most versions of BASIC allow us to refer to the elements of the lists and tables as if they were ordinary variables. This way of handling arrays simplifies array manipulation.

The elements of a list or array can usually be either numeric or string. **Note:** All the elements must be of the same type, either numeric or string but not both. Some versions of BASIC allow strings to be present in lists but not in tables.

Within one program each array must have a unique name, thus no two arrays can share the same letter or letter-dollar sign. If the array is numeric it must be named by a simple letter; if it is a string array it must be named by a letter followed by a dollar sign. Usually array names cannot be subscripted, i.e., letter-integer or letter-integer-dollar sign.

An ordinary variable and an array may share the same name. Unfortunately this becomes rather confusing and is thus not recommended. See *Subscript Variables*.

●**LOAD:** The LOAD command instructs the computer to take an already written program into its memory, usually from tape or disc. The LOAD command typically requires an argument, usually the name of the program desired.

EXAMPLES:
LOAD,MATH-TEST
LOAD,SPACE-WARS

● **LOC:** See *Random Data Files Pointer Control.*

● **LOF:** See *Random Data Files Pointer Control.*

● **LOG:** The library function LOG returns the natural (Base E) logarithm of the argument in parentheses.

EXAMPLE:
```
10    PRINT LOG(J)
20    Q = LOG(J/K)
```

PROGRAMMING EXAMPLE:
```
10    REM THIS PROGRAM DEMONSTRATES
20    REM THE LOG FUNCTION
30    PRINT "ENTER A BASE AND AN ARGUMENT"
40    INPUT J,K
50    IF J = 0 OR K = 0 THEN 80
60    PRINT LOG(K)/LOG(J)
70    GOTO 30
80    END
```

RUN

```
ENTER A BASE AND AN ARGUMENT
?10,5
0.69897
ENTER A BASE AND AN ARGUMENT
?2,4
2
ENTER A BASE AND AN ARGUMENT
?1.34, 8.96
7.49231
ENTER A BASE AND AN ARGUMENT
?0,0
END
```

● **LONG:** In some versions of BASIC double precision mathematics and variables are allowed. To indicate that a variable is a double

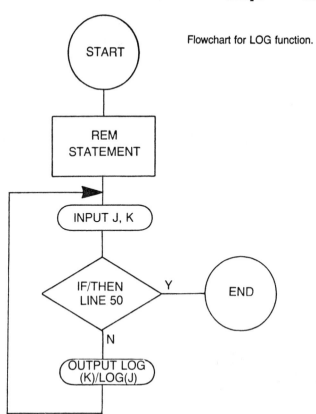

Flowchart for LOG function.

precision variable, the variable name is preceded by the keyword LONG on a line prior to the use of the variable in a function. Typically, double precision produces 12 digit variables. If a variable is indicated to be double precision, any operation on that variable will also produce a double precision output. If an assignment is required, the variables on both sides of the equal sign must be indicated as being double precision.

EXAMPLE:

```
10    LONG J
20    LONG K
30    PRINT LOG(J)
40    LET K = SQR(J)
```

● **Loops:** It is often necessary to write a program in which the same portions are performed not just once but a number of times.

Where a given action is done a multitude of times, a programming device named the LOOP is used in order to write a simplified program using as few statement lines as possible.

To demonstrate the simplicity and shortness of the loop technique, two sample programs will be given. Both will solve the same problem, but the latter will use the loop technique.

Let's assume we need a table of the first 100 numbers plus their natural logs. Without a loop technique the program would be written as follows:

```
10      PRINT 1, LOG(1)
20      PRINT 2, LOG(2)
30      PRINT 3, LOG(3)
40      .........
        .........
        .........
970     PRINT 97, LOG(97)
980     PRINT 98, LOG(98)
990     PRINT 99, LOG(99)
1000    PRINT 100, LOG(100)
1010    END
```

The above program would require 101 lines of code. Yet using the loop technique only five lines are required.

```
10      LET J = 1
20      PRINT J, LOG(J)
30      LET J = J + 1
40      IF J < = 100 THEN 20
50      END
```

By using the FOR-TO statement we can further cut down the number of lines to four.

```
10      FOR J = 1 TO 100
20      PRINT J, LOG(J)
30      NEXT J
40      END
```

We can also have loops within loops. See *Nested Loops.*

●**Machine Language:** Machine language is the actual list of instructions that the computer understands. All computer languages, including BASIC, are translated into the machine language of the computer being used by its compiler.

A program written on one computer will therefore run on another computer (assuming we are using the same language, such as BASIC, LISP or other high-level language) but the languages themselves will only run on the same type of computer. There are so many versions of BASIC, for example, because each and every different computer requires that the language be written in its own machine codes.

●**MARGIN:** The MARGIN statement consists of the keyword MARGIN followed by a variable or a number. This statement controls or changes the maximum line length produced by output statements to "N" characters. When "N" is reached, an automatic carriage return/line feed is generated. That is, except for the difference in line length the output operation remains the same.

EXAMPLE:

```
10    MARGIN N
20    MARGIN K—J
30    MARGIN 72
```

●**MAT CON:** The MAT CON is used to assign a value of one to each element of a given matrix.

EXAMPLE:

```
10    MAT J = CON
```

(where J is a matrix previously dimensioned).

Example of the MAT CON statement:

$$J = \begin{bmatrix} 1 & 1 & 1 \\ 1 & 1 & 1 \end{bmatrix}$$

●**MAT IDN:** The MAT IDN statement assigns a value of zero to each element of a square matrix (Z × Z matrix) except those elements on the principal diagonal. The principal diagonal is the diagonal that runs from upper left to lower right, and a value of one will be assigned to each of its elements.

A matrix that is assigned these values is known as an identity matrix.

EXAMPLE:

10   MAT J = IDN

(where J is a square matrix that has been previously dimensioned).

The identity matrix has an important characteristic: if a square matrix K is multiplied by the identity matrix J, then the product will be the square matrix K.(K*J = J*K = K).

Example of an Identity Matrix:

$$J = \begin{bmatrix} 1 & 0 & 0 \\ 0 & 1 & 0 \\ 0 & 0 & 1 \end{bmatrix}$$

●**MAT INPUT (Matrix):** Some versions of BASIC allow the MAT INPUT statement to enter matrix elements as well as vector elements. With a matrix, however, the number of data elements to be entered must always be specified with the MAT INPUT statement.

● **MAT INPUT (Vector):** The MAT INPUT statement in BASIC is used to enter vector elements directly from an input terminal.

EXAMPLE:

10   MAT INPUT J

Most versions of BASIC only allow one vector to appear in a MAT INPUT statement.

When the MAT INPUT statement is executed by the computer a question mark (?) will appear at the start of a new line, indicating a request for data. Execution of the program will be suspended until the user types in the required vector elements, separated by commas. The first element entered will be assigned to J(1), the second to J(2), and so forth (assuming that J is the vector name). The zeroth element of the vector will be ignored.

After the user has finished entering the data, the user must depress the RETURN key, indicating to the computer to continue execution.

Any number of elements may be entered provided that the number of data elements does not exceed the maximum number of vector elements, as specified by the DIM statement for that particular vector name.

If the number of data elements is too great for one line, subsequent lines may be used if each line to be extended ends in an ampersand (&). The ampersand must therefore appear after the last data element in each line except the last. A new question mark will be printed at the start of a new line if the ampersand was used to terminate the previous line.

EXAMPLE:

?1,4,−5,8,9,−23,4,18,28&
?8,7,−2,17,8,11,−10,19,30,47

If the vector was dimensioned for 50 elements and only 20 elements have been entered, the vector elements X(21) to X(50) will not be affected by the MAT INPUT statement.

PROGRAMMING EXAMPLE:

```
10    REM THIS PROGRAM DEMONSTRATES THE
20    REM MAT INPUT STATEMENT
30    DIM K(100),J(100)
40    PRINT "ENTER K VALUES"
50    MAT INPUT K
60    LET K1 = NUM
70    PRINT "ENTER J VALUES"
80    MAT INPUT J
90    LET J1 = NUM
100   IF K1 < > J1 THEN 130
110   PRINT "THE NUMBER OF J AND K ELEMENTS ARE
      THE SAME"
120   GOTO 170
130   IF K1 > J1 THEN 160
140   PRINT "THERE ARE MORE J ELEMENTS THAN K
      ELEMENTS"
150   GOTO 170
160   PRINT "THERE ARE MORE K ELEMENTS THAN J
      ELEMENTS"
170   END
```

Flowchart for MAT INPUT statement.

● **MAT INV:** If we inverse a square matrix we generate a square matrix for which the product and its inverse are equal to the identity matrix.

Therefore, if J is the original matrix and K is its inverse we have:

$$J*K = K*J = L$$

where L is the identity matrix.

A matrix must be square for its inverse to be defined, but it is not possible to calculate an inverse for all matrices that are square.

To calculate the inverse, if it exists, we use that MAT INV statement.

EXAMPLE:

10   MAT J = INV(K)

(where K is the original matrix and J is assigned the inverse of K. Both J and K must be previously dimensioned.)

● **MAT PRINT:** In BASIC the MAT PRINT statement is used to print the elements of a vector or a matrix.

EXAMPLE:

10   MAT PRINT J
20   MAT PRINT K

In the previous examples, J and K may either be vectors or matrices. The elements of J for example will be printed in columnar form if J is a vector, and in table form if J is a matrix. As with the MAT READ statement, the zeroth elements will be ignored. When the MAT PRINT statement is operating on a matrix, each element of each row will be widely spaced, wtih a maximum of 5 elements per line. Therefore, in the cases of large matrices, several lines may be required for each row. A blank line will appear between successive rows.

The following rules always apply:

A) MATRICES

    1) Following a matrix name with a comma will have no effect on the spacing of the output.

    2) Following a matrix name with a semicolon will cause the elements of the rows of the matrix to be printed with a minimum of spacing between the elements. Successive rows will be separated by a blank line.

B) VECTORS

    1) If a vector name is followed by a comma, then the elements will be printed in row form rather than columnar form. Wide separation (maximum 5 elements per row) will be used.

    2) If a vector name is followed by a semicolon, then the elements of the vector will be printed in row form with minimum spacing between them.

Several vectors or matrices can appear in the same MAT PRINT statement if desired. Array names must be separated by commas or semicolons. The output will be determined by the type of punctuation following each array name.

The MAT PRINT statement can contain only matrix and vector names. Function references and formulae are not permitted.

The following are valid MAT PRINT statements:

```
10      MAT PRINT A
20      MAT PRINT A,
30      MAT PRINT A;
40      MAT PRINT A,B
50      MAT PRINT A;B
60      MAT PRINT A,B;
70      MAT PRINT A;B;
80      MAT PRINT A,B,K;J;
```

● **MAT READ:** In BASIC the MAT READ statement is used to enter values for the elements of a vector or matrix. This statement is used in conjunction with DATA statements.

EXAMPLE:

```
10      MAT READ K
```

(where K is a vector or matrix that has already been dimensioned).

    When the computer executes a MAT READ statement, the set of elements in the DATA statements are assigned to the elements of the matrix beginning with the subscript 1.

    In versions of BASIC that permit a zero subscript the elements with subscript zero will be ignored. That is, the following elements will not be assigned values from a MAT READ statement: $Y(0,0)$, $Y(X,0)$, $Y(0,X)$. Therefore, whenever using matrices in a version of BASIC that allows zero subscripts, never use them, as the first element in a vector or matrix is always 1, not 0.

A single MAT READ statement may contain more than one matrix or vector.

EXAMPLE:

10   MAT READ X, Y, Z

(where X, Y, Z are previously dimensioned).

● **MAT TRN:** In BASIC the MAT TRN statement causes the rows and columns of a given matrix to be interchanged or transposed.

EXAMPLE:

10   MAT(J) = TRN(K)

(where K is an M × N matrix and J is the generated N × M matrix. Both J and K must be previously dimensioned.)

The elements are related as follows:

$J(I,L) = K(L,I)$

and matrix J is termed the transpose of the Matrix K.

EXAMPLE:

$$\text{If } K = \begin{bmatrix} 1 & 8 & 10 \\ 4 & 7 & 3 \end{bmatrix}$$

then 10 MAT J = TRN(K) will generate

$$J = \begin{bmatrix} 1 & 4 \\ 8 & 7 \\ 10 & 3 \end{bmatrix}$$

As we can see the Nth row of K becomes the Nth column of J and the Nth column of K becomes the Nth row of J.

● **MAT ZER:** In BASIC the MAT ZER statement is used to assign a value of zero to each element of a given matrix.

EXAMPLE:

10   MAT J = ZER

(where J is a matrix previously dimensioned).

Example of the MAT ZER statement:

$$J = \begin{bmatrix} 0 & 0 & 0 \\ 0 & 0 & 0 \end{bmatrix}$$

●**Matrix Addition:** To carry out matrix addition the MAT addition statement form is used.

EXAMPLE:

10   MAT K = J + L

The result of this MAT statement is that each element of K is assigned the sum of the corresponding elements of J and L. Thus K(1,3) = J(1,3) + L(1,3).

Note: The two matrices being added must have the same number of rows and columns.

If J and L are both 2×3 matrices, whose elements are

$$J = \begin{bmatrix} 1 & 3 & 5 \\ 2 & 4 & 6 \end{bmatrix} \qquad L = \begin{bmatrix} 3 & 5 & 1 \\ 2 & 3 & 4 \end{bmatrix}$$

the MAT statement

10   MAT K = J + L

will cause K to be a 2×3 matrix whose elements are

$$K = \begin{bmatrix} 4 & 8 & 6 \\ 4 & 7 & 10 \end{bmatrix}$$

A matrix may be updated by the following procedure,

10 MAT K = K + J

but multiple sums are not permissible; that is,

10   MAT K = K + J + L

would not be allowed.

●**Matrix Assignment:** To assign the matrix A to matrix B the MAT assignment statement is used.

EXAMPLE:

```
10     MAT J = K
20     MAT L = P
30     MAT H = G
```

In the case of MAT J = K, each element of K is assigned to the corresponding element of J.

Thus if K is the following 2×3 matrix

$$K = \begin{bmatrix} 1 & 5 & 8 \\ -4 & 6 & -9 \end{bmatrix}$$

the statement

```
10     MAT J = K
```

will cause J to be a 2×3 matrix whose elements are

$$J = \begin{bmatrix} 1 & 5 & 8 \\ -4 & 6 & -9 \end{bmatrix}$$

To reference any element in J we use subscript variables. Thus the value 6 would have been referenced as J(2,2).

●**Matrix Multiplication:** Two matrices may be multiplied if the number of columns in the first matrix is the same as the number of rows in the second matrix. The result of matrix multiplication is the generation of a matrix having the same number of rows as the first matrix and the same number of columns as the second matrix.

Therefore,   if K is a 3×5 matrix and J is a 5×9 matrix,   then the operation L = K*J will generate the L matrix having three rows and 9 columns.

Each element of L will be obtained as follows:

$$L(I,M) = K(I,1)*J(1,M) + K(I,2)*J(2,M) + K(I,3)*J(3,M)$$

Matrix multiplication is carried out in the following statement:

```
10     MAT L = K*J
```

Note: A matrix cannot be updated by means of the matrix multiplication statement.

●**Matrix Subtraction:** The matrix subtraction statement and the matrix addition statement are very similar except for the sign of operation. Thus the matrix subtraction statement takes the form:

10   MAT K = J−L

Each element of K is assigned the difference of the corresponding values of J and L. Therefore:

$$K(1,3) = J(1,3) - L(1,3)$$

The two matrices must have the same number of rows and columns.

If J and L are both 2×3 matrix whose elements are:

$$J = \begin{bmatrix} 1 & 3 & 5 \\ 2 & 4 & 6 \end{bmatrix} \qquad L = \begin{bmatrix} 3 & 5 & 1 \\ 2 & 3 & 4 \end{bmatrix}$$

The MAT statement

10 MAT K = J − L

will cause K to be a 2×3 matrix whose elements are:

$$K = \begin{bmatrix} -2 & -2 & 4 \\ 0 & 1 & 2 \end{bmatrix}$$

A matrix may be updated as follows:

10   MAT K = K−J

●**MID$:** The library function MID$ occurs in two types, one with two arguments and the other with three arguments.

A) Two argument MID$ returns characters from the string expression X$ starting at character position N.

B) Three argument MID$ returns M characters from the string expression X$ starting at Nth character.

EXAMPLES:

```
10     PRINT MID$(X$,N)
20     PRINT MID$(J$,4)
30     PRINT MID$(K$,N,M)
40     PRINT MID$(K$,11,4)
```

PROGRAMMING EXAMPLE:

```
10    REM THIS PROGRAM DEMONSTRATES
20    REM THE MID$ FUNCTION
30    INPUT J$
40    FOR N = 1 TO LEN(J$)
50    PRINT MID$(J$,N,1), MID$(J$,N,2)
60    NEXT N
70    END
```

RUN

```
?BASIC
B    BA
A    AS
S    SI
I    IC
C    C
```

END

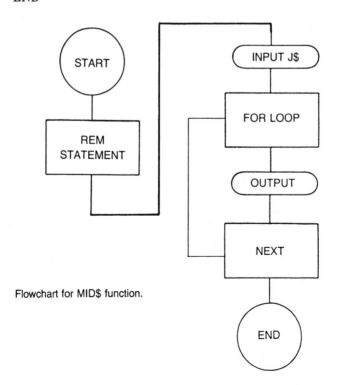

Flowchart for MID$ function.

●**Mode:** In BASIC, mode may be thought of as a description of a switch. Changing the mode is comparable to rotating or toggling a switch to a different position. Each position changes the way a certain operation will be carried out. In the trig functions, mode refers to which format is being used: radians, grads or degrees. The SET command is the controller of the "mode" switch. If we set radians, all trig functions following the SET command (SET RAD) will be in radians.

●**Multiline Functions:** Many calculations cannot be carried out using a single statement, as when lengthy formulae or conditional branching operations are to be carried out. The multiline function format is ideally suited for calculations, complex or lengthy. Like a single line function, a multiline function can have any number of dummy arguments but can return only one value.

The format is as follows: the first statement must be a DEF statement but, unlike a single line function, the multiline function definition is not included in the DEF statement. The last statement must be the FNEND (function end) statement, and consists merely of the keyword FNEND.

Between the DEF and FNEND statements any number of other statements may occur, but at least one must be an assignment statement (LET).

EXAMPLE:

```
10    DEF FNC(J,K,L)
20    ..........
30    ..........
40    LET FNC = (J*K*L)/J–K
50    FNEND
```

The grammatical rules are the same as those for the single line function·

1) A function definition can appear anywhere in a program.
2) A function is referenced by specifying its name, followed by a list of arguments enclosed in parentheses and separated by commas.
3) Control cannot be transferred between a statement within a function and a point external to the function.

The function reference may be nested, with the level of nesting depending on the version of BASIC being used.

EXAMPLE:

```
10     DEF FNZ(J,K)
20     LET FNZ = J
30     IF J < K THEN 50
40     LET FNZ = K
50     FNEND
60     ..........
70     ..........
80     ..........
90     PRINT FNZ(FNZ(A,B),FNZ(B,C))
```

Variables other than those specified as arguments may appear in a multiline function, just as they may be found in a single line function.

●**Multiple Branching:** In BASIC the ON-GOTO statement carries out the function of multiple branching. This statement includes a variable or a formula and a list of remote statements. Control is passed to the first remote statement if the variable or formula equates to 1, to the second if the variable or formula is equal to 2 and so forth.

EXAMPLE:

```
10     ON J GOTO 100, 350, 900, 45
20     ON K—J GOTO 46, 18, 28
30     ON B*A GOTO 1000, 1500, 3010
```

If the variable or formula has a value that is not integral, then the decimal portion will be truncated. **Note:** Many versions of BASIC allow the interchange of keywords GOTO and THEN.

EXAMPLE:

```
10     ON J*K THEN 150, 200, 100, 260
```

PROGRAMMING EXAMPLE:

```
10     REM THIS PROGRAM DEMONSTRATES THE
20     REM ON-GOTO STATEMENT
30     PRINT "ENTER 1 FOR SQUARE ROOT, 2 FOR"
40     PRINT "LOG, 3 FOR SINE AND 4 FOR COSINE"
50     PRINT "ENTER ARGUMENT AFTER OPTION"
60     INPUT J,K
70     ON J GOTO 80, 100, 120, 140
80     LET L = SQR(K)
```

```
 90    GOTO 150
100    LET L = LOG(K)
110    GOTO 150
120    LET L = SIN(K)
130    GOTO 150
140    LET L = COS(K)
150    PRINT
160    PRINT "SOLUTION IS ";L
170    END
```

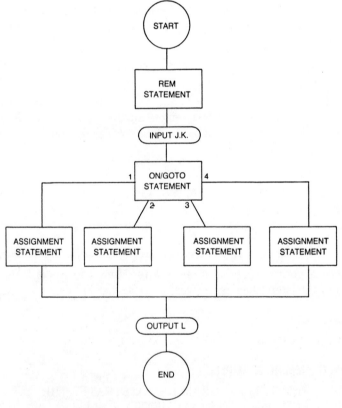

Flowchart for ON/GOTO statement.

●**Nested Loops:** If desired, loops may be nested; that is, one loop may be imbedded within another. In fact, there can be several layers of nesting. The number of layers or levels of nesting depends on the version of BASIC being used.

When writing nested loops, the restrictions applying to the FOR-TO-NEXT loop apply, plus the following requirements:

1) Each nested loop must begin with its own FOR-TO statement and end with its own NEXT statement.
2) An outer loop and an inner (nested) loop cannot have the same running variable.
3) Loops cannot overlap. An inner loop must be totally nested or imbedded within an outer loop.
4) Control can be transferred from a nested loop to a statement in an outer loop or to a remote statement completely outside the nest. However control cannot be transferred from a remote statement outside the nest into the nest.

EXAMPLE:

```
10    FOR J = 1 TO K
20    .........
30    .........
40    FOR L = 1 TO M
50    .........
60    .........:.
70    NEXT L
80    NEXT J
```

PROGRAMMING EXAMPLE:

```
10    REM THIS PROGRAM DEMONSTRATES
20    REM THE FOR TO NESTED LOOP
30    LET K = 4
40    LET J = 3
50    LET L = 2
60    LET M = 10
70    LET N = 20
80    FOR A = 1 TO 10
90    PRINT A*K
100   FOR B = 1 TO 5
110   PRINT B*J
120   FOR C = 1 TO 5
130   PRINT ((M*N) + L)/C
140   NEXT C
150   NEXT B
160   NEXT A
170   END
```

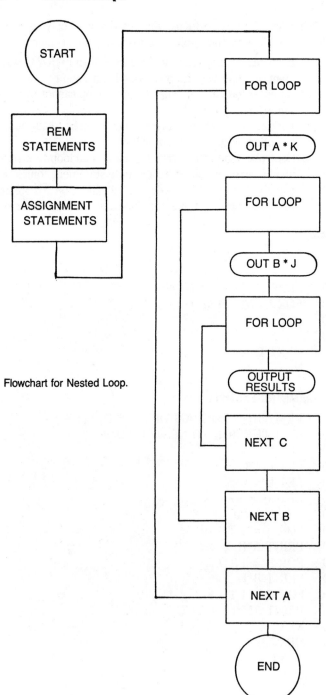

Flowchart for Nested Loop.

●**NEW:** NEW is a system command that is entered without a line number during command mode. The NEW command clears the workspace in the computer's main memory and prepares it for a new program.

Depending on the version of BASIC being used, the computer may respond with a query such as "NEW PROGRAM NAME—". After the user supplies the name, the computer will type out READY.

●**NOT:** The NOT statement is used in conjunction with the IF THEN statement. It is written as follows:

10   IF NOT J THEN 600

If J is equal to zero then the statement is true; if J is equal to any positive or negative number the statement is false and the branch to 600 will not occur.

PROGRAMMING EXAMPLE:

```
10    REM THIS PROGRAM DEMONSTRATES
20    REM THE NOT FUNCTION
30    PRINT "ENTER 3 NUMBERS, 1 OF WHICH SHOULD BE
      ZERO"
40    INPUT J,K,L
50    IF NOT J THEN 80
60    PRINT "THE FIRST NUMBER IS NOT ZERO"
70    GOTO 90
80    PRINT "THE FIRST NUMBER IS ZERO"
90    IF NOT K THEN 120
100   PRINT "THE SECOND NUMBER IS NOT ZERO"
110   GOTO 130
120   PRINT "THE SECOND NUMBER IS ZERO"
130   IF NOT L THEN 160
140   PRINT "THE THIRD NUMBER IS NOT ZERO"
150   GOTO 170
160   PRINT "THE THIRD NUMBER IS ZERO"
170   END
```

RUN

ENTER 3 NUMBERS, 1 OF WHICH SHOULD BE ZERO
?11,0,−8
THE FIRST NUMBER IS NOT ZERO

THE SECOND NUMBER IS ZERO
THE THIRD NUMBER IS NOT ZERO

END

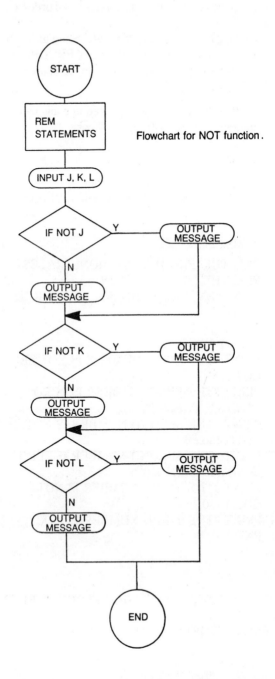

Flowchart for NOT function.

●**NUM:** The NUM function is used to determine how many values have been entered via a MAT INPUT statement. Whenever the library function NUM is referenced, it returns the number of data elements entered only by the most recent MAT INPUT statement. An argument for this function is not required.

EXAMPLE:

```
10    LET J(0) = NUM
20    PRINT J(0);"ELEMENTS"
```

As can be seen by the above example, it is convenient to use the zero element of the vector in the assignment statement using the NUM function.

PROGRAMMING EXAMPLE:

```
10    REM THIS PROGRAM DEMONSTRATES THE
20    REM NUM FUNCTION
30    DIM M(100),N(100)
40    PRINT "ENTER M VALUES"
50    MAT INPUT M
60    LET M1 = NUM
70    PRINT "ENTER N VALUES"
80    MAT INPUT N
90    LET N1 = NUM
100   IF M1 < > N1 THEN 130
110   PRINT  "THE NUMBER OF M AND N ELEMENTS IS
      THE SAME
120   GOTO 170
130   IF M1 > N1 THEN 160
140   PRINT  "THERE ARE MORE N ELEMENTS THAN M
      ELEMENTS"
150   GOTO 170
160   PRINT  "THERE ARE MORE M ELEMENTS THAN N
      ELEMENTS
170   END
```

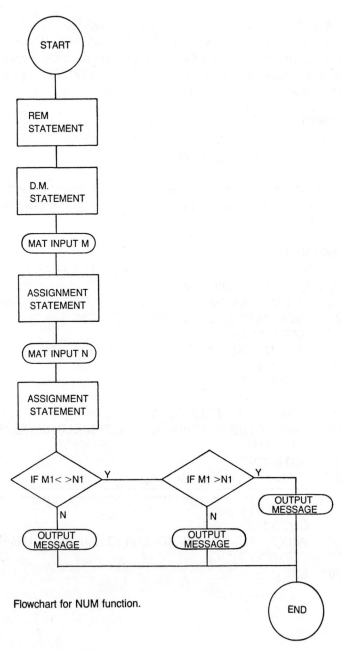

START

REM
STATEMENT

D.M.
STATEMENT

MAT INPUT M

ASSIGNMENT
STATEMENT

MAT INPUT N

ASSIGNMENT
STATEMENT

IF M1< >N1 — Y →   IF M1 >N1 — Y →

N   N

OUTPUT
MESSAGE   OUTPUT   OUTPUT
MESSAGE   MESSAGE

Flowchart for NUM function.

END

● **Numbers:** Numerical quantities in BASIC may be referred to as *constants* or *numbers*. Constants can be expressed as integers or decimals.

The following rules always apply in BASIC:

1) Usually only 8 or 9 significant figures are allowed.
2) A constant may be prefixed with a − or + sign. If no sign is present, the quantity is assumed to be positive.
3) A comma must never appear in any constant.
4) A constant may contain an exponent.
5) Typically constants may range from 10^{-99} through 0 to 10^{99}.

Examples: (each row is valid)

0	+0	-0
1	+1	0.1E + 1
+2000	2000	2.0E + 3
-2500	-2.5E + 3	-.25E + 4
+.125	1.25E-1	125E-3
100000	1E5	1E + 5

●**ON-GOSUB:** In BASIC, the ON-GOSUB statement carries out the function of multiple branching to subroutines. This statement includes a variable or a formula and a list of remote GOSUBs. The first subroutine is called if the variable or formula equals 1, the second if the variable or formula is equal to 2, and so forth.

EXAMPLE:

```
10   ON J GOSUB 100,350,900,45
20   ON K-J GOSUB 46,18,28
30   ON B*A GOSUB 1000,1500,3010
```

If the variable or formula has a value that is not integral, the decimal portion will be truncated.

PROGRAMMING EXAMPLE:

```
10    REM THIS PROGRAM DEMONSTRATES
20    REM THE ON-GOSUB STATEMENT
30    PRINT "ENTER A NUMBER FROM 1 TO 4"
40    INPUT J
50    IF J < 1 OR J > 4 THEN 170
60    ON J GOSUB 90,110,130,150
70    PRINT K
80    GOTO 30
90    K = J*10
100   RETURN
```

```
110    K = J/10
120    RETURN
130    K = EXP(J)
140    RETURN
150    K = LOG(J)
160    RETURN
170    END
```

RUN

ENTER A NUMBER FROM 1 TO 4
?1
10
ENTER A NUMBER FROM 1 TO 4
?2
0.20000
ENTER A NUMBER FROM 1 TO 4
?3
20.0855
ENTER A NUMBER FROM 1 TO 4
?4
1.38629
ENTER A NUMBER FROM 1 TO 4
?5
END

●**ON-GOTO:** See *Multiple Branching.*

●**Operating Commands:** After initializing BASIC in whatever method is required for the computer system being used, BASIC will usually respond with some sort of prompting symbol. This prompting symbol or word indicates that the language is waiting for a command. The following are a list of typical operating (system) commands.

OLD: . . . . . Loads a previously saved program. BASIC may request the name of the old program or file

NEW: . . . . . Allows the user to write a new program. BASIC may request a name for the program or file.

LIST: . . . . . Prints the current program.

RUN: . . . . . Executes the current program.

SAVE, RESAVE or REPLACE: . Saves the current program.

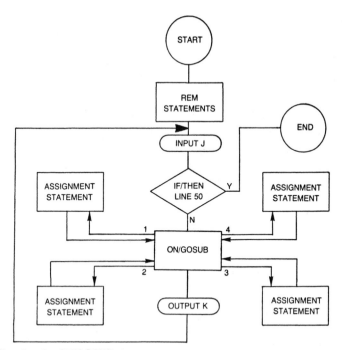

Flowchart for ON/GOSUB statement.

UNSAVE, PURGE
or SCRATCH: . . . . . Deletes the current program
BYE, GOODBYE
or SYSTEM: . . . . . Exit from BASIC

●**Operators:** Operators are special reserved symbols used by BASIC to indicate arithmetic operations.

These operators are:

Addition	$+$
Subtraction	$-$
Multiplication	$*$
Division	$/$
Exponentiation	↑ or ∧ (in some BASICS **)

Operators are used between numbers and numeric variables. Using operators in conjunction with numeric variables and numbers we can generate formulae.

EXAMPLES:

J + K

Q $\uparrow$ R*(Z − 2)

X1-Z-B4

Z*(Z-1)/4

18-4

●**OR:** The OR statement is used in conjunction with the IF THEN statement. It allows the IF THEN statement to have two or more qualifiers instead of one. The IF THEN is true if both qualifiers are true or if either is.

EXAMPLE:

10   IF X = 10 OR Y = 15 THEN 600

In the above example, either the first qualifier (X = 10) or the second (Y = 15) or both must be true if the branch to 600 is to occur.

PROGRAMMING EXAMPLE:

```
10    REM THIS PROGRAM DEMONSTRATES THE
20    REM OR STATEMENT
30    LET K = 10
40    LET J = 20
50    LET L = 30
60    IF K = J/2 OR L = K + J THEN 80
70    STOP
80    IF J = L − K OR J = K*2 THEN 100
90    STOP
100   IF K = 10 OR J = 20 OR L = 30 THEN 120
110   STOP
120   END
```

●**Parentheses:** Parentheses are used to alter the normal hierarchy of operations in a formula. Since parentheses may be nested, they are evaluated from the innermost set outwards. Inside each pair of parentheses, the normal hierarchical status is kept.

Note: Parentheses must always be used in pairs. Any imbalance between number of left and right parentheses will cause an error condition.

For example, to evaluate the algebraic formula

$$[3.14(K + J)^5 + (19Y)^3] \, K/(J + 9)$$

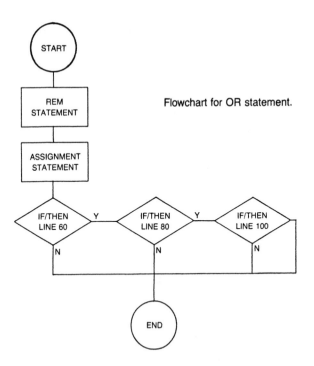

Flowchart for OR statement.

it may be written in BASIC as

$$(3.14*(K + J) \uparrow 5 + (19*Y) \uparrow 3) \uparrow (K/(J + 9))$$

The introduction of extra parentheses in an equation will do no harm, but obviously the formula that uses the minimum number of parentheses is easier to read.

●**Password:** Some computer systems (usually large installations) require the user to enter a password to allow him access to the computer's facilities. The password may be numeric, a string or a combination thereof. An illegal password will not allow the user to operate or use the computer.

EXAMPLE:

PASSWORD?
KEN
READY

In the above example the password was accepted, but in the following the wrong password was used.

EXAMPLE:

PASSWORD?
PETER
ILLEGAL PASSWORD, TRY AGAIN
PASSWORD?

Generally the computer will allow the user three to four tries. After the fourth try, if the proper password has not been entered the connection to the terminal is turned off.

●**PEEK:** The PEEK and POKE commands allow the user of BASIC to write and read machine code instructions. Thus while running BASIC the programmer may write a machine language program by using the POKE command; using the PEEK command

Flowchart for PEEK function.

the programmer can read back the machine codes. To run the machine language instructions the CALL statements is used.

The PEEK function in BASIC returns the contents of memory address (J). The value returned will be equal to or greater than 0 and less than or equal to 255. J must be in the range of 0 to 65535.

EXAMPLE:

```
10    PRINT PEEK(J)
20    PRINT PEEK(2819)
```

See *CALL*.

PROGRAMMING EXAMPLE:

```
10    REM THIS PROGRAM DEMONSTRATES
20    REM THE PEEK FUNCTION
30    FOR I = 300 TO 310
40    PRINT PEEK(I)
50    NEXT I
60    END
```

● **PI:** The library function PI returns the value of 3.1415926. It requires no argument.

EXAMPLE:

```
10    PRINT PI
20    PRINT PI*A
30    J = PI*K
```

● **POKE:** The PEEK and POKE commands allow the user of BASIC to write and read machine code instructions. Thus while running BASIC the programmer may write a machine language program by using the POKE command; using the PEEK command the programmer can read back the machine codes. To run the machine language instructions the CALL statements are used.

The POKE statement stores the byte specified by its second argument (J) into the location given by its first argument (K). The byte to be stored must usually be equal to or greater than zero and less than or equal to 255. The location usually lies between zero and 65535. K and J must be separated by commas.

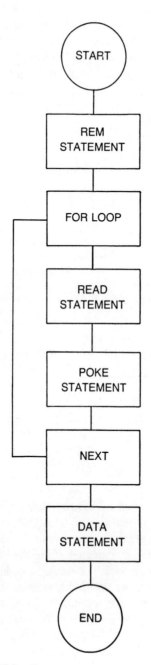

Flowchart for POKE function.

EXAMPLES:

```
10    POKE K,J
20    POKE 2560,130
30    POKE K, 250
```

Note: POKE stores directly into main memory. Care must be taken to see that important data is not over-written by the POKE statement.

See *CALL*.

PROGRAMMING EXAMPLE:

```
10    REM THIS PROGRAM DEMONSTRATES THE
20    REM POKE FUNCTION
30    FOR I = 4001 TO 4010
40    READ N
50    POKE I,N
60    NEXT I
70    DATA 11,18,104,206,118,114,100,89,1,10
80    END
```

A program of this type can be used to generate machine language programs and subroutines. Obviously the data items in the DATA statements must correspond to the machine language codes of the machine the BASIC program is running on.

●**Pointers and Counters:** A pointer is used to point to a certain item of data such as the Nth data element in a DATA statement. The pointer keeps track of what data items have been read and at what position we are in the collection of items. See *Random Data Files Pointer Control*. A counter keeps track of how many times an operation has been carried out, the I in the following statement is a counter:

FOR I = 1 TO 10

●**Precision:** Precision is the number of digits used in calculations in BASIC. Typically *single* precision offers 6 to 8 digits of accuracy in mathematical evaluations. *Double* precision offers twice as many digits, while *triple* precision offers three times as many numeric digits. Double or triple precision is used when greater than normal accuracy is required.

EXAMPLES:

Single precision:
345.786   (6 digits total)

Double precision:
6754998.75478   (12 digits total)

Triple precision:
345837658796546784   (18 digits total)

●**PRINT:** The PRINT statement is used to transmit data (numeric or string) to the output device. This statement consists of the key word PRINT and a list of the output data. The output data may be formulae, strings, or variables. Successive items must be separated by either commas or semicolons. Strings must be enclosed in quotation marks.

EXAMPLE:

```
10    PRINT "JANE", "KEN"
20    PRINT X; Y; Z
30    PRINT "HELLO"; A$
40    PRINT 9*X-4
```

The following rules always apply:

1) Each PRINT statement generates only one new line unless the list presented by the PRINT statement requires more than one line.
2) A PRINT statement containing no data items will produce a blank line.
3) In most versions of BASIC, an integer quantity that contains eight or less digits will be printed as an integer number. If an integer quantity exceeds eight digits, it will be rounded to six significant figures and printed as a decimal number with an exponent. A decimal quantity is printed as a decimal number. If the quantity contains more than six digits, it will be rounded to six digits. An exponent will be shown if the magnitude of the number exceeds 999999 or is less than 0.1 and contains more than six significant figures.
4) Strings must always be enclosed in quotation marks.
5) If the data items in a PRINT statement are separated by commas, each line of output will be divided into 5 zones of equal length. One output value will be printed per zone.

6) If a comma follows the last item in a PRINT statement, the first output from a subsequent PRINT statement will be printed on the same line if sufficient space permits.

7) Up to four commas may be placed in a PRINT statement consecutively. The effect of each comma is to space over one zone. With this method widely spaced data may be achieved.

8. If semicolons are used instead of commas to separate data items, no spaces will be left between items.

9) Placing a semicolon after the last data item in a PRINT statement causes the output of the next PRINT statement to occur on the same line without any spaces.

PROGRAMMING EXAMPLE:

```
10    REM THIS PROGRAM DEMONSTRATES THE PRINT
20    REM STATEMENT
30    LET K = 15
40    LET J = 10
```

Flowchart for PRINT statement.

```
50    PRINT
60    PRINT 1, 2, 3, 4, 5
70    PRINT
80    PRINT J, J*2, J*3, J*4, J*5
90    PRINT K, K*2, K*3, K*4, K*5
100   PRINT
110   PRINT "K TIMES J EQUALS"; K*J
120   PRINT "K LESS J EQUALS"; K-J
130   END
```

RUN

1	2	3	4	5
10	20	30	40	50
15	30	45	60	75

K TIMES J EQUALS 150
K LESS J EQUALS 5

END

●**PRINT USING:** The PRINT USING statement allows the user to output multiple fields of both strings and numerics, where the strings are enclosed in quotation marks. The usage can be readily understood by carefully reading the examples.

EXAMPLE:

```
10    LET A = 10.34
20    LET B = 5.06
30    LET C = 9.18
40    A$ = " $$###.## $$###.## $$###.##"
50    PRINT USING A$;A;B;C
```

This example produces the following output:
$10.34 $5.06 $9.18

Of course strings may be added to the PRINT USING statement. If we replace line 40 with:
```
40  A$ = "THE AMOUNTS ARE: (A)##.##, (B)##.##,
              AND (C)##.##"
```
we obtain for an output the following:
THE AMOUNTS ARE: (A)10.34,(B)5.06;AND (C)9.18

Note: The commas, parentheses, numerics (if any) and strings will be reproduced in the output.

Thus we can see that the PRINT USING statement allows formatting of the output. It allows control over justification and spacing of the output.

PROGRAMMING EXAMPLE:

```
10    REM THIS PROGRAM DEMONSTRATES
20    REM THE PRINT USING FUNCTION
30    LET J = 4.15
40    PRINT USING "####.##",J,"BACTERIA"
50    LET J = J*3
60    IF J > 340 THEN 80
70    GOTO 40
80    END
```

Flowchart for PRINT USING statement.

RUN

    4.15 BACTERIA
   12.45 BACTERIA
   37.35 BACTERIA
  112.05 BACTERIA
  336.15 BACTERIA

END

● **Program:** A program may be defined as a set of directions or instructions that tell a computer how to solve a problem. Any program (written in BASIC or any other computer language) must fulfil certain requirements.

    1) It must be written in a language that is understood by the computer.
    2) It must be written completely and precisely. A computer has no way to interpret what you "really" mean; it can only do what you tell it to do.

Regardless of the language being used, or the type of computer system being run on, each and every program consists of three basic sections:

    1) The necessary information, the input data
    2) Processing of the input data
    3) Output of the results obtained from the processing.

As with any formalized procedure, if mistakes occur in the program, you will undoubtedly end up with something other than desired for the output.

● **?(Question Mark):** See *PRINT*.

● **QUOTE:** The QUOTE Statement is used to indicate to the BASIC program that the information being stored in a file is to be enclosed in quotation marks and will be read back at some time in the future by a BASIC program.

EXAMPLE:

10   QUOTE
20   QUOTE #2

In line 20 of the above example, the #2 signifies that there is more than one set of information and that the quote refers to the second set only.

QUOTE: See *Sequential Data Files Writing*.

● **Random Data Files:** A random data file contains individual data items that are not arranged in any particular order. With a random data file each data item can be read directly from, or written directly onto, without proceeding sequentially along the data file from the beginning. Thus random is faster.

Note: Random data files may consist of either string or numeric data but not both. The type of random file is specified with either a percent sign (%) for numeric files or the dollar sign ($) for string files. Usually a positive integer quantity (generally ranging from one to 132) must follow the $ sign. The positive integer quantity specifies the maximum number of characters that may appear in each string.

Random data files, unlike sequential data files, cannot be listed directly on a terminal device. The BASIC system commands cannot edit a random data file, but of course we can easily write a program which will handle the above two problems.

● **Random Data File Creation:** Typically BASIC does not have system commands which can create a file. Therefore we must write a special BASIC program to create a random data file.

EXAMPLE:

```
10    FILES COUNTRIES $20
20    INPUT J$
30    IF J$ = "END" THEN 60
40    WRITE:1,J$
50    GOTO 20
60    END
```

Before the program is run, the user must type in NEW. The computer will respond with NEW FILE NAME, and the user types in the new name. Then the user must type in SAVE. After the program is RUN the user must type SAVE again.

● **Random Data Files Pointer Control.** The data items in a random data file are not arranged in any special order, but the locations of the data items are numbered sequentially from the start of the file (beginning with number one) and are incremented by one for each consecutive data item. The concept of a pointer is used to indicate the location of any particular data file. The pointer must always be properly positioned before a data item can be transferred to or from (read or write) the data file.

EXAMPLE:

LOCATION	DATA ITEM
1	301049
2	21659
3	28
4	10
5	18
6	13718
7	8046
8	2091
9	18461
10	22964

The pointer is automatically advanced one location every time a data item is transferred to or from the data file. Therefore it is also possible to read or write data sequentially from a random data file. By using the SET statement (RESET in some versions of BASIC) we can reposition the pointer at any time.

Two library functions are closely related to the SET statement. They are the LOC and LOF functions. The LOF function indicates the last storage location in the file, while LOC allows us to determine the position of the pointer.

When using the SET statement we must also indicate which data channel is being used.

The format is to have the keyword SET followed by a colon (as opposed to % in sequential files), followed by the channel number, then the location. The location may be specified by a formula, a variable, or a numeric constant, and must be separated by a comma from the channel number.

EXAMPLE:

```
10    SET:1,J
20    SET:3,4
```

● **Random Data File Reading:** In BASIC a random data file can be read either sequentially or randomly. The pointer position need not be considered if the data is to be read sequentially because the FILES statement places the pointer at the first location in the file and automatically advances one location each time a new data item is read.

If the items in a data file are to be read randomly, we must position the pointer to the proper location with the SET statement before attempting to read a particular data item.

EXAMPLE:

Sequential

```
10    FILES COUNTRIES$20
20    FOR M = 1 TO Z
30    READ:1,J$
40    PRINT J$
50    NEXT M
60    END
```

Random

```
10    FILES COUNTRIES$20
20    PRINT "LOCATION IN FILE"
30    INPUT K
40    SET:1,K
50    READ:1,J$
60    PRINT J$
70    GOTO 20
80    END
```

● **Random Data Files Reset Command:**   See *Random Data Files Pointer Control.*

● **Random Data Files Set Command:**   See *Random Data Files Pointer Control.*

● **Random Data File Writing:** In the same manner that a data item is read, a data item can be written onto a random file. Whereas with reading we use the READ statement, with writing we use the WRITE statement. The pointer must be positioned to the proper location before an entry can be written; also the new data item will replace the old data item previously stored in that location.

EXAMPLE:

```
10    FILES COUNTRIES$20
20    PRINT "WHICH LOCATION"
30    INPUT K
40    PRINT "DATA IS"
50    INPUT J$
60    SET:1,K
70    WRITE:1,J$
80    GOTO 20
90    END
```

●**RANDOMIZE:** The numbers generated by the RND library function are not truly random, as they are produced by a fixed computational procedure. However, they do have the same statistical properties as do numbers which are truly random in nature. Numbers produced by random number generators are usually called pseudo-random numbers.

Every time a program which uses the RND function is run the same sequence of random numbers will be generated. For purposes of debugging, this reproducibility feature is very helpful, but most users would usually want different numbers each time the program is run.

The RANDOMIZE statement is used to ensure that a different sequence will be generated each time the program is run. The RANDOMIZE statement consists simply of the keyword RANDOMIZE. This function operates by providing a different starting point for the random number generator. Thus the RANDOMIZE statement must precede the first reference to the RND library function.

EXAMPLE:

```
10     DIM K(50)
20     RANDOMIZE
30     ..........
40     FOR I = 1 TO 50
50     LET K(I) = RND
60     NEXT I
```

PROGRAMMING EXAMPLE:

```
10     REM THIS PROGRAM DEMONSTRATES
20     REM THE RANDOMIZE FUNCTION
30     RANDOMIZE
40     DIM J(100)
50     FOR I = 1 TO 100
60     J(I) = RND
70     NEXT I
80     FOR I = 1 TO 100
90     PRINT J(I)
100    NEXT I
110    END
```

●**READ-DATA:** When large numbers of data items are to be entered into the computer, the standard INPUT statement may be used, but this process can become time-consuming and tends to introduce errors. In such a case, the READ-DATA statement would be preferable. The READ-DATA statement is also the only way to introduce data in TIMESHARING and SINGLE-USER MODES.

The READ statement specifies the variables whose values are to be entered into the computer via the program. This statement consists of the keyword READ followed by a list of input variables separated by commas. The list can contain ordinary numeric and/or string, or subscripted variables representing numeric and/or string.

The purpose of the DATA statement is to assign the appropriate values to the variables listed in the READ statement. The DATA statement consists of the keyword DATA followed by the list of numbers and/or strings, separated by commas. Of course each data entry in the DATA statement must correspond to the variable in the READ statement.

EXAMPLE:

```
10     READ L, K$, J$, X
20     DATA 100, KEN, JAYN, 150
```

All DATA statements regardless of their position in the program form a single DATA block. Each item in the DATA block maps (or corresponds) on a one to one basis to an appropriate variable in the READ statements. Actually this is not a true one to one correspondence as you may have more variables on one line of a READ statement than on one line of a DATA statement.

It should also be pointed out that in the following examples line 10 and line 20 are identical to line 30.

EXAMPLE:

```
10     DATA 5, HELLO, 36, 84
20     DATA FOX, HUNT, 82
30     DATA 5, HELLO, 36, 84, FOX, HUNT, 82
```

It is also to be remembered that the DATA specified by the READ-DATA statement are an integral part of the program as opposed to the INPUT statement.

Thus no matter how often the same program is run, the same data remains.

The following rules must be observed with a DATA block:

1) The DATA items must correspond in order (mapping) and in type to the variables specified by the READ statement.

2) There must be at least as many data elements in the DATA block as there are variables in the READ statements. Extra data will be ignored.

3) The elements in a DATA statement must be separated by commas. The last item in the DATA statement is *not* followed by a comma.

4. Elements of a DATA statement must be numeric or string in nature, not variables or formulae.

5. Strings containing commas or beginning or ending with blank spaces must be enclosed in quotation marks.

6) DATA statements should (but do not have to) be placed consecutively near the end of the program.

PROGRAMMING EXAMPLE:

```
  5   REM DEMONSTRATES READ/DATA STATEMENTS
 10   READ K,J,L,M
 15   LET H = K*M-J*L
 20   IF H = 0 THEN 65
 30   READ P,Q
 40   LET X = (P*M-J*Q)/H
 45   LET Y = (K*Q-P*L)/H
 50   PRINT X,Y
 60   GOTO 30
 65   PRINT "NO UNIQUE SOLUTION"
 70   DATA 1,2,4
 80   DATA 2,-7,5
 90   DATA 1,3,4,-7
100   END
```

● **READY:** A BASIC generated message indicating that the computer is waiting for a user command.

● **Relational Operators:** Relational operators are used to carry out conditional branching, allowing a branch to occur under certain well defined conditions.

The following is the list of relational operators:

$=$ equal to

$<>$ not equal to (Some BASICs use #)

$<$ less than

$>$ greater than

$<=$ less than or equal to

$>=$ greater than or equal to

See *Conditional Branching.*

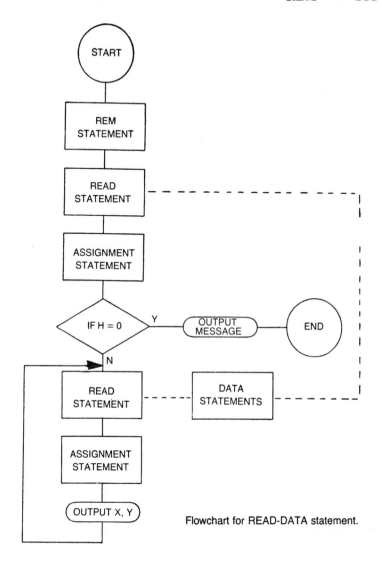

Flowchart for READ-DATA statement.

● **REM:** The REM statement provides no executable instructions for the computer. The chief reason for the use of REM statements is to properly document a program as it is the easiest way to introduce remarks (comments) into a BASIC program. This statement consists of the keyword REM and the message.

EXAMPLE:

10   REM THIS IS A PROGRAM

Rem statements can be placed anywhere in a BASIC program. In some versions of BASIC it is also possible to include a remark on the same line as an ASSIGNMENT statement. To separate the remark from the rest of the statement an apostrophe must precede the remark.

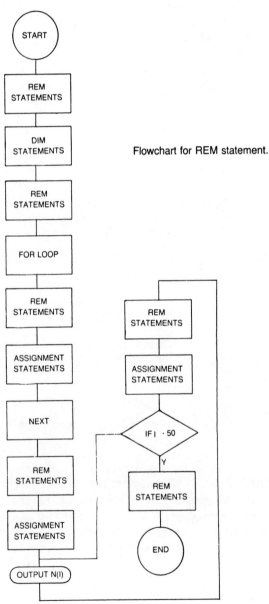

Flowchart for REM statement.

EXAMPLE:

```
10    LET K = J*A 'CALCULATE 1ST PRODUCT
```

PROGRAMMING EXAMPLE:

```
10    REM THIS PROGRAM DEMONSTRATES
20    REM THE REM STATEMENT
30    REM DIMENSION VARIABLE N
40    DIM N(50)
50    REM SET N(1 −50) = 1-50
60    REM IN A FOR LOOP
70    FOR I = 1 TO 50
80    REM SET VALUE OF N(I)
90    LET N(I) = I
100   NEXT I
110   REM PRINT OUT N(1-50)
120   REM USING A GOTO LOOP
130   LET I = 1
140   PRINT N(I)
150   REM INCREMENT I
160   LET I = I + 1
170   IF I > 50 THEN 190
180   GOTO 140
190   REM PROGRAM TERMINATES
200   END
```

● **RENAME:** The RENAME or REN command allows the user to rename a program that is contained currently in the computer's main memory work space.

The computer will generally respond to "RENAME" with "NEW PROGRAM NAME—", and the user then supplies the new name.

● **RESET:** See *Random Data Files Pointer Control.*

● **RESTORE:** The correspondence between variables in the READ statement and the elements in the DATA statement is maintained by an internal pointer. The internal pointer indicates the next data element in the list to be read. In the case of strings and numerics there are two pointers, one for each. Every time a data element is read the pointer is incremented.

If the data has to be read again, whether it be some of the data or all of it, the RESTORE statement is used. The RESTORE statement consists of the keyword RESTORE only. The use of this statement is to restore the pointer or pointers to the first data element or elements.

EXAMPLE:

```
10      READ J,K,L
20      ..........
30      ..........
40      RESTORE
50      READ M,N,P,Q
60      ..........
70      ..........
80      RESTORE
90      READ R,S
100     ..........
110     DATA 2,4,6,8,10,12,14
```

In the example given, J, K, L are assigned the values of the first three elements. Using the RESTORE statement we can assign to M, N, P, Q the first four values. If the RESTORE statement in line 80 was not present M, N, P, Q would have been assigned the "next" four values.

In most versions of BASIC using the RESTORE statement, an asterisk (*) or dollar sign ($) may be placed directly after the RESTORE keyword.

The asterisk indicates to the computer to restore only the numeric pointer, while the dollar sign indicates to restore only the string pointer.

EXAMPLE:

```
10      READ X,Y,Z,J$,K$
20      ..........
30      ..........
40      RESTORE*
50      READ H,I
60      ..........
70      ..........
80      READ L$
90      ..........
100     RESTORE $
110     READ A$,B$
120     ..........
130     DATA 10,20,30,MOUSE,RACCOON, SQUIRREL
```

In this example X, Y, Z are assigned 10, 20, 30. H and I are assigned 10, 20 because of the RESTORE* in line 40. J\$ and K\$ are assigned MOUSE and RACCOON, then in line 80 L\$ is assigned SQUIRREL. Since the RESTORE\$ was not encountered until line 100, L\$ was assigned the next string value. In line 110 A\$ and B\$ are assigned MOUSE and RACCOON, because this READ statement follows the RESTORE\$ statement.

● **RESUME:** See *CONTINUE*.

● **RETURN:** The RETURN statement closes the subroutine procedure. When the computer encounters the keyword RETURN, control is transferred back to the statement following the point of reference. The RETURN statement consists of only the keyword RETURN.

Note: Control cannot be returned to the point of calling by other types of branching statements.

EXAMPLE:

```
10     LET K = 10
20     LET J = 20
30     GOSUB 80
40     ..........
50     PRINT Z
60     ..........
70     ..........
80     LET Z = J-K
90     RETURN
```

● **RIGHT\$:** The library function RIGHT\$ returns the rightmost N characters of the string expression X\$

EXAMPLES:

```
10     PRINT RIGHT$(X$,N)
20     PRINT RIGHT$(K$,6)
```

● **RND:** In BASIC, the RND library function is used to generate a random number. This function will return a different random number, with a value between zero and one, each time the function is referenced. Generally an argument is not required, but in some versions of BASIC, typically the integer-only versions, an argument is required. The RND function will then generate integer random numbers from 0 to the value of the argument.

EXAMPLE:

```
10     DIM K(50)
20     ..........
30     ..........
40     FOR I = 1 TO 50
50     LET K(I) = RND
60     NEXT I
```

The above example will generate 50 random numbers. It should be remembered that the random function never generates a one, but a value very close to one.

To generate a randon number between X and Y, the following formula may be used:

$$LET\ Z = X + (Y-X)*RND$$

EXAMPLE:

```
10     LET K = RND(J)
20     LET H = RND(10)
30     LET J = RND(28)
```

PROGRAMMING EXAMPLE:

```
10     REM THIS PROGRAM DEMONSTRATES
20     REM THE RND FUNCTION
30     PRINT "THIS PROGRAM ROLLS DICE"
40     LET J = INT(6*RND) + 1
50     LET K = INT(6*RND) + 1
60     PRINT "THE DICE ARE ":J;" AND ";K
70     END
```

● **RUN:** RUN is a typical command in BASIC; it is not a statement. Once the program under consideration has been entered or loaded, the user types in RUN and the program is executed. If a compiler form of BASIC is used, the program is compiled first then run.

Note: After all commands, it is generally necessary to hit the return key to signal to the computer that you have finished entering a command or data, and that it should proceed.

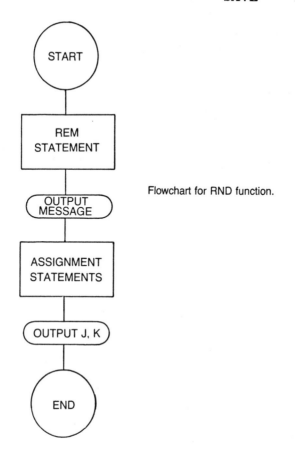

Flowchart for RND function.

Some versions allow entering RUN with a number following it. In this case, the program execution will commence at the line number specified.

● **SAVE:** After writing a program in BASIC the user can keep the program either on tape or on disc by using the SAVE command. The SAVE command usually requires the name of the program as an argument. Depending on the version of BASIC being used the user may be limited to the number of letters used in the name.

EXAMPLE:

SAVE,HEATLOSS
SAVE,INSULATION-FACTOR

After saving the program by name, the user can request the already written program by using the LOAD command.

●**Scalar Multiplication:** If all the elements of a given matrix are multiplied by a given constant, we say that the operation of scalar multiplication is being carried out.

EXAMPLE:

10   MAT K = (J)*L

K and L are matrices, and J is an ordinary variable. Each element of K will be defined as K(I,J) = (J)*L(I,J).

If L is the following 2 × 3 matrix:

$$L = \begin{bmatrix} 1 & 3 & 5 \\ 2 & 4 & 6 \end{bmatrix}$$

and J = 2, then 10 MAT K = (2)*L where the elements of K are:

$$K = \begin{bmatrix} 2 & 6 & 10 \\ 4 & 8 & 12 \end{bmatrix}$$

The term within the parentheses need not be a single variable. Subscripted variables, constants, formulae and function references may all be used, as long as the term represents a single numerical quantity. The scalar term must always be enclosed in parentheses.

The following are all valid scalar multiplication statements:

10   MAT K = (25)*L
20   MAT J = (Z*Y)*H
30   MAT L = (SQR(H-P))*B

Updating with scalar multiplication is as follows:

10   MAT K = (J)*K

● **SCRATCH:** The SCRATCH (SCR) command clears or erases the current contents of the computer's main memory work space but returns the current program name.

●**Sequential Data Files:** A sequential data file contains data sets that are arranged in the order of increasing line numbers. A sequential data file generally consists of several lines of data, with each line beginning with a line number. The data items in any given line may be numbers, strings, or a combination of the two. Data items must be separated by either commas or blank spaces. If a string contains commas or blank spaces it must be enclosed in quotation marks. See also *Files* and *Random Data Files*.

● **Sequential Data File Creation:** Since a sequential data file is structured almost precisely in the same way as a BASIC program, we can generally create and edit a sequential file in the same manner as a program. We can also print a sequential data file on a terminal.

● **Sequential Data File Reading:** In most applications, the information or data stored in a sequential data file will be read and then processed by a BASIC program. The data items in a sequential data file must be read in the same order that they are stored in, starting at the beginning of the sequential data file.

Note: All the information that is read will be retained for subsequent use.

There are three fundamental file manipulation statements: FILES, INPUT and IF END.

Transfer of information between a BASIC program and the data file always takes place over a data channel. The keyword FILES assigns the data file NAME to data channel #X. This must be done prior to any information transference to or from the data file.

Therefore, all subsequent file statements will refer to the data file by channel number, not by name. The keyword INPUT reads from the data file sequential information. The keyword IF END tests for the end of the data file.

EXAMPLE:

```
10    FILES DATES
20    INPUT #1, K,J$,Z$
30    PRINT K,J$,Z$
40    IF END #1 GOTO 60
50    GOTO 20
60    END
```

● **Sequential Data File Writing:** A BASIC program may write information onto a data file, much in the same manner as information is read from a sequential data file. Because sequential data files *are* sequential, new information or data will automatically be written beyond any existing data. This obviously protects any information already stored.

If the old data is to be deleted prior to the writing of new data, then the old data file must explicitly be erased and repositioned to its starting point.

The fundamental statements used in writing a data file are FILES QUOTE, SCRATCH, INPUT, PRINT, and IF END.

The FILES statement must always be prior to any other file manipulation statement. Once the data files have been assigned to their respective data channels, all references to these files will use the channel number *not* the file name. If a file statement contains N names, the data channels are assigned 1 to N reading left to right after the keyword FILE.

EXAMPLE:

10   FILE STATUS, QUEUE, SAVING

(In this example, file "status" is channel #1, file "queue" is channel #2, and "savings" is #3.)

The keyword QUOTE specifies that all strings written into a particular data file will be enclosed in quotation marks. This is important if the strings are to be read subsequently by a BASIC program.

EXAMPLE:

10   QUOTE #3

The keyword SCRATCH causes a particular file to be erased and reset to its starting point, in preparation for writing new data.

EXAMPLE:

10   SCRATCH #1

The keyword PRINT instructs the computer to print the variables listed after the file PRINT statement from the file pointed to by the channel number following the keyword PRINT.

EXAMPLE:

10   PRINT #3,Z,T$,J$

● **SET:** The SET statement is usually used to set different modes of operation within the BASIC interpreter or compiler. The following are examples of different modes that are affected by the SET statement.

  1) SET RADIAN: sets trigonometric functions to radian mode.
  2) SET DEGREE: sets trigonometric functions to degree mode.
  3) SET GRAD: sets trigonometric functions to grad mode.

4) SET TRACE: sets trace mode, which in most versions of BASIC prints out the line numbers as they are being executed. This function is very useful in debugging.

5) SET NORMAL: cancels the SET TRACE function.

Of course, depending on the version of BASIC being used, there may or may not be SET statements, or different ones than those shown here.

EXAMPLE:

```
10    SET RADIANS
20    Y COS(X)
30    SET DEGREE
40    Z COS(X)
50    SET GRAD
60    K COS(X)
```

See also *Random Files Pointer Control.*

● **Set Pointer:** See *Random Data Files Pointer Control.*

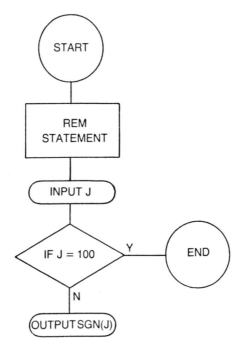

Flowchart for SGN function.

● **SGN:** The library function SGN returns a one if the argument is positive (greather than zero), a zero if the argument is equal to zero, and minus one if the argument is negative (less than zero).

EXAMPLE:

```
10    PRINT SGN(10)
20    PRINT SGN(0)
30    PRINT SGN(-45)
40    PRINT SGN(K*J)
```

PROGRAMMING EXAMPLE:

```
10    REM THIS PROGRAM DEMONSTRATES
20    REM THE SGN FUNCTION
30    PRINT "ENTER ANY NUMBER"
40    INPUT J
50    IF J = 100 THEN 80
60    PRINT SGN(J)
70    GOTO 30
80    END
```

RUN

```
ENTER ANY NUMBER
?0
0
ENTER ANY NUMBER
?-234
-1
ENTER ANY NUMBER
?28
1
ENTER ANY NUMBER
?100

END
```

● **SIN:** The library function SIN returns the sine of the expression X, where X is in parentheses. X is interpreted as being in radians.

EXAMPLE:

```
10     PRINT SIN(J)
20     PRINT SIN(Q)
30     Q = SIN(K)
```

PROGRAMMING EXAMPLE:

```
10     REM THIS PROGRAM DEMONSTRATES
20     REM THE SIN FUNCTION
30     FOR I = 1 TO 5
40     PRINT SIN(I)
50     NEXT I
60     END
```

RUN

0.84147
0.90929
0.14112
-0.75680
-0.95892

END

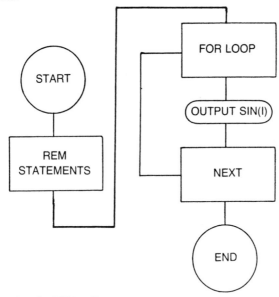

Flowchart for SIN function.

● **Slash:** See *Colon*.

● **Space (Available):** To check for how much relative space you have available for programs try the following program:

```
10    DIM J(K)
20    FOR I = 1 TO K
30    LET J(I) = J(I) + 1
40    NEXT I
50    END
```

Try different values of K until you receive a "OUT OF MEMORY" error message.

● **SPACE$:** The SPACE$ Function returns a string of spaces, the length being specified by the numeric formula, constant or variable (truncated to an integer) in parentheses following the keyword SPACE$.

EXAMPLE:

```
10    SPACE$(10)
20    SPACE$(J)
30    SPACE$(J*K)
```

● **SQR:** The library function SQR returns the square root of the argument in parentheses. X must be greater than or equal to zero.

EXAMPLE:

```
10    PRINT SQR(Q)
20    K = SQR(J)
```

PROGRAMMING EXAMPLE:

```
10    REM THIS PROGRAM DEMONSTRATES
20    REM THE SQR FUNCTION
30    FOR I = 10 TO 100 STEP 10
40    PRINT SQR(I)
50    NEXT I
60    END
```

RUN

```
3.16227
4.47214
5.47722
6.32456
```

7.07107
7.74597
8.36667
8.94427
9.48683
10.0000

END

Flowchart for SQR function.

●**STATUS:** The STATUS or STA command is usually associated with large computer systems. After the user types in the STATUS command during command mode, the computer will respond with the following:

    A) The current program name
    B) The current data and time
    C) The amount of CPU time the user has used since LOGON.

●**STEP:** See *FOR-TO*.

● **STOP:** The STOP statement is used in BASIC to halt program execution. In effect it is a GOTO statement to the END statement.

    The STOP statement can be used more than once and anywhere within the structure of a program. The END statement, as opposed to the STOP, must only be used once—at the end of the program.

PROGRAMMING EXAMPLE:

```
10    REM THIS PROGRAM DEMONSTRATES THE STOP
20    REM STATEMENT
30    LET Z = 10
40    LET X = 5
50    LET Y = 2
60    IF Z = 10 THEN 80
70    STOP
80    IF Z = X*Y THEN 100
90    STOP
100   IF Z = X-Y THEN 120
110   STOP
120   IF Z = X THEN 60
130   END
```

● **STR$:** The library function STR$ returns a string which is the character representation of the numeric expression X.

EXAMPLE:

```
10    PRINT STR$(18.9)                        ("18.9")
```

● **String:** A string is a sequence of characters (alphanumeric plus special characters such as +, −, /, *, $...etc.). A blank space may be included in a string, but never quotation marks because quotation marks are delimiters and mark the beginning and the end of a string. The maximum number of characters any string may have will depend

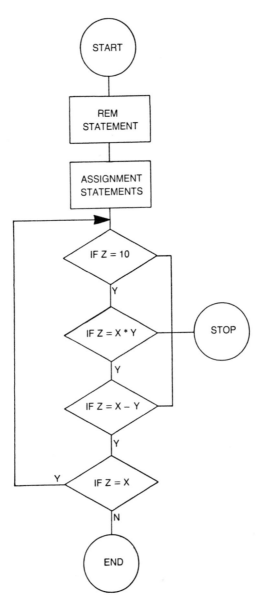

Flowchart for STOP statement.

on the version of BASIC being used. The function of a string is to represent such non-numeric data as labels, messages, etc.

Note: A sequence of integers in a string does not represent a numeric data.

Flowchart for String manipulation.

EXAMPLES:

"BASIC"
"THIS IS A STRING"
"THE DATE IS"
"TYPE YES TO RESTART"
"$153.92"
"301019491621959"

PROGRAMMING EXAMPLE:

```
10    REM THIS PROGRAM DEMONSTRATES STRING
20    REM MANIPULATION
30    PRINT "TYPE ANY FOUR LETTERS"
40    INPUT J$(1),J$(2),J$(3),J$(4)
50    FOR M = 1 TO 4
60    FOR N = 1 TO 4
70    IF N = M THEN 140
80    FOR P = 1 TO 4
90    IF P = M THEN 130
100   IF P = N THEN 130
110   LET R = 10-(M + N + P)
120   PRINT J$(M); J$(N); J$(P); J$(R)
130   NEXT P
140   NEXT N
150   NEXT M
160   END
```

● **Subroutines:** A subroutine is a program within a program that does a predefined function. Sometimes it is easier and more useful to structure such a procedure as a subroutine than as a function. Subroutines, like functions, may be referenced from different points within a program. Whereas a function is given a name, a subroutine is not; it is referenced by the line number of the first statement of the subroutine. A subroutine can determine more than one numeric and/or string quantity and arguments are not required. Thus a subroutine may be viewed as a very generalized function.

A subroutine may be called from different points in the program by the GOSUB and the ON-GOSUB commands. The first statement within the subroutine structure may be of any type, but the last statement must always be the keyword RETURN. A subroutine may have more than one RETURN statement, as for multiple or conditional branching procedures.

The advantage of the subroutine structure is the ability to write a section of code once, yet use it in many places in the same program, which saves a lot of memory, especially if the subroutine is large and it is called several times. If a subroutine contains 10 lines of statements and is called six times we can save 38 lines of code. Why 38? Every subroutine must end in a return statement; thus the routine itself is only nine lines long. We have six calls statements, nine lines of routine, and one return, or 16 lines total. If all nine lines had been written six times throughout the program 54 lines would have been required.

● **Subscripted Variables:** The individual elements within an array are known as subscripted variables. Any element in an array can be referred to by using the array name followed by the value of the subscript in parentheses. With lists, only one subscript is required; with tables, two subscripts are needed to properly identify any given element.

The subscripts may be variables, numbers, or formulae. The following are valid subscript variables:

K(J)
L(M)
H(1,5)
Z(K1, J1)
P(ABS(X-4), ABS(X + 4))

Note: The variable, or formula written within the parentheses, will be truncated if it has a value that is non-integer. If the value is negative, an error message will be generated and program execution will be halted.

Subscript variables may be used just as ordinary variables within a program.

By placing subscript variables within loops and using either counter techniques or the FOR-TO loop technique, we can refer to the elements in the array with ease. **Note:** Remember the running variable of the FOR-TO statement may be used within the loop as long as its value is not changed.

● **System Commands:** See *User Commands.*

● **TAB:** The library function TAB spaces to a specified position on the printer or video terminal. It must be used in conjunction with a print statement. The TAB function specifies the absolute position from the left hand margin where printing is to start.

EXAMPLE:

10   PRINT TAB(J)

PROGRAMMING EXAMPLE:

```
10    REM THIS PROGRAM DEMONSTRATES
20    REM THE TAB FUNCTION
30    FOR I = 1 TO 5
40    PRINT TAB(J)"BASIC"
50    NEXT I
60    END
```

RUN

```
BASIC
 BASIC
  BASIC
   BASIC
    BASIC
```

END

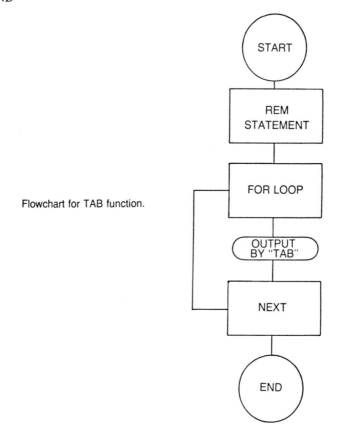

Flowchart for TAB function.

●**TAN:** The library function TAN returns the tangent of the argument in parentheses, interpreted as being in radians.

EXAMPLE:

```
10    PRINT TAN(J)
20    K = TAN(J)
```

PROGRAMMING EXAMPLE:

```
10    REM THIS PROGRAM DEMONSTRATES
20    REM THE TAN FUNCTION
30    FOR I = 1 TO 5
40    PRINT TAN(I)
50    NEXT I
60    END
```

RUN

```
1.35741
-2.18503
-0.14254
1.15782
-3.38052
```

END

●**TEXT:** The TEXT or TEX command is used in conjunction with the versions of BASIC that have graphics capabilities. The command TEXT sets the video output back to standard text mode (alphanumerics plus the standard symbols).

●**THEN:** See *GOTO*.

●**TIM:** To find the amount of time required to run a program the TIM function may be used. The TIM function requires a dummy argument in parentheses. The value given by TIM is processor time, in seconds, used since the RUN command was given to the computer.

EXAMPLE:

```
10    PRINT "TIME = "; TIM(X)
```

●**USER:** See *CALL*.

●**User Commands:** User Commands are commands such as RUN, LOAD, SAVE, LIST. These are commands that are independent of the program being run concurrently. User Commands are often termed *System Commands*.

Flowchart for TAN function.

●**VAL:** The library function VAL returns the string expression X$ converted to a number. If the first non-space character of the string is not a plus or minus sign, a digit, or a decimal point, then a zero will be returned.

EXAMPLE:

10	PRINT VAL(J$)	
20	PRINT VAL("123.4")	(123.4)

●**VARIABLES:** A string or numeric constant may be represented by a name called a variable. In most versions of BASIC each numeric variable must consist of a letter or a letter followed by an integer. A string variable must be written as a letter followed by a dollar sign, ($). **Note:** Most BASIC versions allow string variables to be written as a letter, an integer, then the dollar sign.

EXAMPLES:

I	J	K1	J2	X4	Z9
I$	J$	K1$	J2$	X4$	Z9$

● **Vector and Matrix Operations:** MATRIX and VECTOR are mathematical terms that are in reference to a table and a list respectively. A one-dimensional array is called a vector, while a two-dimensional array is termed a matrix (plural to matrices). A vector is therefore only a special type of matrix, and thus most of the rules that apply to matrices apply to vectors.

The individual elements of the array are represented by subscript variables. When dealing with matrices the subscript variable requires two subscripts, for example $J(K,L)$, where K represents the row and L the column. Thus $J(5,8)$ is the element found in the fifth row and eighth column of the matrix J. If a matrix has K rows and L columns it is referred to as a $K \times L$ matrix.

In most versions of BASIC a subscript has a preset value of 10. If a greater value is required a DIM statement must be used.

The operations of addition, subtraction, scalar multiplication and vector multiplication are the most common vector and matrix operations.

Appendices

DERIVED FUNCTIONS

The following functions which are not typical of standard BASIC library functions may be easily implemented by the following formulae:

ARC SIN(X) = ATN(X/SQR(X*X + 1))
ARC COS(X) = ATN(X/SQR(X*X + 1)) + 1.5708
ARC SEC(X) = ATN(SQR(X*X −1)) + (SGN(X) − 1)*1.5708
ARC CSC(X) = ATN(1/SQR(X*X) − 1)) + (SGN(X) − 1)*1.5708
ARC COT(X) = −ATN(X) + 1.5708
ARC SINH(X) = LOG(X + SQR(X*X + 1))
ARC COSH(X) = LOG(X + SQR(X*X − 1))
ARC TANH(X) = LOG((1 + X)/(1 − X))/2
ARC SECH(X) = LOG((SQR(X*X + 1) + 1)/X)
ARC CSCH(X) = LOG((SGN(X)*SQR(X*X + 1) + 1)/ X)
ARC COTH(X) = LOG((X + 1/(X − 1))/2
COT(X) = 1/TAN(X)
CSC(X) = 1/SIN(X)
SEC(X) = 1/COS(X)
COSH(X) = (EXP(X) + EXP(− X))/2
COTH(X) = EXP(−X)/(EXP(X) − EXP(− X))*2 + 1
CSCH(X) = 2/(EXP(X) − EXP(−X))
SECH(X) = 2/EXP(X) + EXP(−X))
SINH(X) = (EXP(X) − EXP(−X))/2
TANH(X) = −EXP(−X)/(EXP(X) + EXP(−X))*2 + 1

135

DIAGNOSTICS (COMMON)

READ/RESUME, NO DATA: The user has not provided any DATA statements or data but has used either the READ or RESTORE statements.

FOR, NO NEXT: The user has constructed a FOR-TO loop but has not closed it with a NEXT statement.

UNDIMENSIONED: Variables that were being used as matrices were not dimensioned.

VECTOR + ARRAY: The same variable was used both as a vector and an array.

VALUE OUTSIDE RANGE: A value has exceeded the bounds for that particular function.

GOSUB NESTING: The user has used more levels of GOSUB nesting than the version of BASIC used allows.

RETURN: A RETURN statement was executed before a GOSUB statement.

DIVISION BY ZERO: Division by zero was tried.

INVALID EXPONENT: A**B, where A<0 and B< >INT (B).

LOG(−X): The log of a negative number was specified.

SQR(−X): The square root of a negative number was specified.

OUT OF DATA: The set of DATA elements has been exhausted and a READ statement is executed.

ILLEGAL CONSTANT: A string (numeric) data element is read into a numeric (string) variable.

FUNCTION PREVIOUSLY DEFINED: A user defined function (DEF statement) has been defined more than once in one program.

ARRAY PREVIOUSLY DIMENSIONED: An array or a matrix has been defined more than once in one program.

NO SUCH LINE#: A reference has been made to a nonexistent line number.

FOR NESTING (MAX = X): Where the user has exceeded the maximum of nesting (where X is the maximum for that particular version of BASIC).

NESTING SAME INDEX: Where a user has constructed a nested FOR loop with two or more of the FOR-TO statements using the same running variable (index variable).

WRONG NEXT: The matching NEXT statement must follow the corresponding FOR-TO statement.

ILLEGAL NESTING: FOR-TO loops may be nested, but they must not overlap.

OVERFLOW: A numeric constant exceeds the maximum single-precision floating-point value.

UNDERFLOW: A numeric constant is smaller than the minimum single-precision floating-point value.

MEMORY EXCEEDED: The generated object code exceeds the bounds permitted by the computer and/or the version of BASIC being used.

INCREASE PROGRAM SPEED

1) Use GOSUB sparingly.
2) Minimize GOTOs from one section to another section of the program.
3) Check if FOR-NEXT is faster than or slower than IF-THEN loops.
4) For simple integer multiplication such as 2*K, K+K will be faster.
5) Check whether simple code is faster than or slower than complex expressions.

SAVING SPACE

To conserve space and limit the size of programs the following hints may be implemented.

A) Use multiple statements per line number, if the version of BASIC allows. There is an overhead of about 5 bytes associated with each line in a program.

B) Use integer values whenever possible as opposed to real numbers.

C) Delete all unnecessary spaces from program lines.
EXAMPLE:

```
10    PRINT K, J; L
```
Could be entered as

```
10    PRINTK,J;L
```

D) Use as few REM statements as possible.

E) Use variables rather than constants, when the same constant is required more than a few times.

F) A program that is one loop and is ended by either CTRL C or by running out of data usually does not require an END statement.

G) Re-use variables over and over if possible.

H) Use go-subs instead of repeating lines of code.

SPEED

The following programs may be timed to give an indication of processing speed.

```
10    FOR I = 1 TO 1000
20    LET X = X+1
30    NEXT I
40    PRINT X
50    END
```

Instead of line 20 being LET X = X+1, the user may try 20 LET X = 10*X or 20 LET X = X/10. Multiplication and division are fairly complex software routines. Using the above two replacements will give a fair indication of this type of operation speed.

Index

ABS	17	ELSE	45
AND	18	END	45
Argument	20	EXP	45
Array	20		
ASC	21	Files	47
ASCII	23	FN	47
Assignment	23	FOR-TO	49
ATN	25	FRE	51
Back Slash	26	GOSUB	52
BYE	26	GOTO	54
		Graphical Output	56
CALL	26		
CATALOG	28	Hierarchy	56
CAT	28	HOME	57
CHANGE	28		
CHR$	32	IF-END	57
CLEAR	33	IF-THEN	57
Colon	33	IF-THEN DO, ELSE	57
Concatenation	34	INPUT	57
Conditional Branching	36	INSTR	59
CONTINUE	37	INT	61
Control Characters	38		
COPY	38	LEFT$	63
COS	38	LEN	64
		LENGTH	65
DEF	40	LET	66
DET	42	Library Functions	66
DIM	43	Line Numbers	66
DIMENSION	45	LIST	67
DO END	45	Lists and Tables	67
Dummy Arguments	45	LOAD	67

LOC	68	RANDOMIZE	108
LOF	68	READ-DATA	108
LOG	68	READY	110
LONG	69	Relational Operators	110
Loops	69	REM	111
		RENAME	113
Machine Language	70	RESET	113
MARGIN	71	RESTORE	113
MAT CON	71	RESUME	115
MAT IDN	71	RETURN	115
MAT INPUT (Matrix)	72	RIGHT$	115
MAT INPUT (Vector)	72	RND	115
MAT INV	75	RUN	116
MAT PRINT	75		
MAT READ	76		
MAT TRN	77		
MAT ZER	77	SAVE	117
Matrix Addition	78	Scalar Multiplication	118
Matrix Assignment	79	SCRATCH	118
Matrix Multiplication	79	Sequential Data Files	118
Matrix Subtraction	80	Creation	119
MID$	80	Reading	119
Mode	82	Writing	119
Multiline Functions	82	SET	120
Multiple Branching	83	Set Pointer	121
		SGN	122
Nested Loops	84	SIN	122
NEW	87	Slash	124
NOT	87	Space (Available)	124
NUM	89	SPACE$	125
Numbers	90	SQR	125
		STATUS	126
ON-GOSUB	91	STEP	126
ON-GOTO	92	STOP	126
Operating Commands	92	STR$	126
Operators	93	String	126
OR	94	Subroutines	129
		Subscripted Variables	130
Parentheses	94	System Commands	130
Password	95		
PEEK	96		
PI	97		
POKE	97		
Pointers and Counters	99	TAB	130
Precision	99	TAN	132
PRINT	100	TEXT	132
PRINT USING	102	THEN	132
Program	104	TIM	132
? (Question Mark)	104		
QUOTE	104		
		USER	132
		User Commands	132
Random Data Files	105		
Creation	105		
Pointer Control	105		
Reading	106		
Reset Command	107	VAL	133
Set Command	107	Variables	133
Writing	107	Vector and Matrix Operations	134